CW01368586

Murray Walker's
GRAND PRIX YEAR

Volume 2

Foreword by JACKIE STEWART

Photography JOHN TOWNSEND

PUBLISHED IN ASSOCIATION WITH ICI

ACKNOWLEDGEMENTS

When Roger Chown, the Managing Director of First Formula Publishing, suggested to me in 1986 that we should produce a Grand Prix Year Book dealing with the 1987 season as I'd seen it, I must admit that I was sceptical about its chances of success. 'There are several jolly good ones already,' I said, 'and what's more they are well-established with ready acceptance and a loyal readership. One more would be one too many!'

But he's a persuasive chap is Roger and *Murray Walker's Grand Prix Year* was on sale on 4th December — no mean achievement by the whole team bearing in mind that I didn't arrive back in the UK with the story of the last GP of the year, Australia, until 17th November! My objective had been to produce something concise, informative, accurate and readable. Roger's objective with the help of John Townsend's superb photography and his enthusiastic and capable colleagues at Clifford Frost (notably Geoff Wootton who did a magnificent job with the layout and typography) had been to produce a quality publication which looked good, was acceptably priced and available well before Christmas.

I'm delighted to say that, between us, we seem to have rung the bell, for the book had a really heartening reception and seemed to fill a niche that had been empty before. So we've done it again!

And this year, just as last, I've realised how many kind and helpful friends I've got in the Grand Prix world. In 1987 I paid homage to the ones who had been especially encouraging to me in putting together my first effort of this kind (talking about it is one thing but I rapidly found that writing about it is quite another!) and I thank them again. The Drivers, Team Owners, Managers, Sponsors, Mechanics, Trade and Public Relations Representatives and all the rest of the 'Pit Lane and Paddock Club' — especially including the Media people who dig and delve to find the facts (and rumours!) and my friends at the BBC whose efforts have, I sincerely believe, provided British TV viewers with Grand Prix coverage of unrivalled quality and depth. It would have been even better if we'd had the often-promised but seldom provided in-car cameras which add so much to the appreciation and enjoyment of Grand Prix racing but hopefully we'll have them next year — and maybe compulsory fuel and tyre stops too. Now that would be something!

I would also like to say a special 'thank you' to Jackie Stewart for the generous remarks he makes in the Foreword to this book.

Because of all these fine people you are holding this account of a momentous Formula One World Championship Year — the last of the Turbos — and one which once again demonstrated that there's no more colourful, impactful and exciting Sport than Grand Prix Racing. I hope you like it.

Murray Walker

Publisher's note

The publishers would like to acknowledge the help given by *The Marlboro Grand Prix Guide*, Steven Tee (for his picture of Jackie Stewart), Stuart Sykes and Ann Bradshaw, Ruth Kinnear, Martin Whitaker, Isabelle Magnillat, the ICI team, and finally Lee Gaug, Barry Griffin and Chris Leese, all of Goodyear, whose friendship and hospitality at Grand Prix events, kept the editor in reasonable shape.

Published by First Formula Publishing, an imprint of First Frost Ltd, in association with ICI
First published 1988
© *Murray Walker 1988*
ISBN 1 870066 09 X (P/B)
     1 870066 10 3 (H/B)

Edited by Roger Chown. Designed by Geoff Wootton.
Typeset, printed and produced by
Clifford Frost Ltd, Lyon Road, Wimbledon SW19 2SE.
Colour reproduction by Sinclair Graphics.
All rights reserved.

Contents

Formula One Grand Prix Statistics	4	Race Seven — France	61
Foreword	5	Race Eight — Great Britain	69
1988 Drivers — Picture Gallery	6	Race Nine — Germany	77
Drivers, Teams and Cars 1988 Season	8	Race Ten — Hungary	85
Preface	9	Race Eleven — Belgium	93
Race One — Brazil	13	Race Twelve — Italy	101
Race Two — San Marino	21	Race Thirteen — Portugal	109
Race Three — Monaco	29	Race Fourteen — Spain	117
Race Four — Mexico	37	Race Fifteen — Japan	125
Race Five — Canada	45	Race Sixteen — Australia	133
Race Six — USA East	53	Review of 1988	141

FORMULA ONE GRAND PRIX RACE STATISTICS TO 1987

DRIVERS' WORLD CHAMPIONSHIP

1950 Giuseppe Farina, ITA (Alfa Romeo)
1951 Juan-Manuel Fangio, ARG (Alfa Romeo)
1952 Alberto Ascari, ITA (Ferrari)
1953 Alberto Ascari, ITA (Ferrari)
1954 Juan-Manuel Fangio, ARG (Maserati/Mercedes)
1955 Juan-Manuel Fangio, ARG (Mercedes)
1956 Juan-Manuel Fangio, ARG (Lancia/Ferrari)
1957 Juan-Manuel Fangio, ARG (Maserati)
1958 Mike Hawthorn, GB (Ferrari)
1959 Jack Brabham, AUS (Cooper-Climax)
1960 Jack Brabham, AUS (Cooper-Climax)
1961 Phil Hill, USA (Ferrari)
1962 Graham Hill, GB (BRM)
1963 Jim Clark, GB (Lotus-Climax)
1964 John Surtees, GB (Ferrari)
1965 Jim Clark, GB (Lotus-Climax)
1966 Jack Brabham, AUS (Brabham-Repco)
1967 Denis Hulme, NZ (Brabham-Repco)
1968 Graham Hill, GB (Lotus-Ford)
1969 Jackie Stewart, GB (Matra-Ford)
1970 Jochen Rindt, AUT (Lotus-Ford)
1971 Jackie Stewart, GB (Tyrrell-Ford)
1972 Emerson Fittipaldi, BRA (Lotus-Ford)
1973 Jackie Stewart, GB (Tyrrell-Ford)
1974 Emerson Fittipaldi, BRA (McLaren-Ford)
1975 Niki Lauda, AUT (Ferrari)
1976 James Hunt, GB (McLaren-Ford)
1977 Niki Lauda, AUT (Ferrari)
1978 Mario Andretti, USA (Lotus-Ford)
1979 Jody Scheckter, SA (Ferrari)
1980 Alan Jones, AUS (Williams-Ford)
1981 Nelson Piquet, BRA (Brabham-Ford)
1982 Keke Rosberg, FIN (Williams-Ford)
1983 Nelson Piquet, BRA (Brabham-BMW)
1984 Niki Lauda, AUT (McLaren-TAG/Porsche)
1985 Alain Prost, FRA (McLaren-TAG/Porsche)
1986 Alain Prost, FRA (McLaren-TAG/Porsche)
1987 Nelson Piquet, BRA (Williams-Honda)

CONSTRUCTORS' WORLD CHAMPIONSHIP

1958 Vanwall
1959 Cooper
1960 Cooper
1961 Ferrari
1962 BRM
1963 Lotus
1964 Ferrari
1965 Lotus
1966 Brabham
1967 Brabham
1968 Lotus
1969 Matra
1970 Lotus
1971 Tyrrell
1972 Lotus
1973 Lotus
1974 McLaren
1975 Ferrari
1976 Ferrari
1977 Ferrari
1978 Lotus
1979 Ferrari
1980 Williams
1981 Williams
1982 Ferrari
1983 Ferrari
1984 McLaren
1985 McLaren
1986 Williams
1987 Williams

GP WINS

28 Alain Prost
27 Jackie Stewart
25 Jim Clark
25 Niki Lauda
24 Juan-Manuel Fangio
20 Nelson Piquet
16 Stirling Moss
14 Jack Brabham
14 Emerson Fittipaldi
14 Graham Hill
13 Alberto Ascari
13 Nigel Mansell
12 Mario Andretti
12 Alan Jones
12 Carlos Reutemann
10 James Hunt
10 Ronnie Peterson
10 Jody Scheckter

Others
7 René Arnoux
6 Ayrton Senna
5 Michele Alboreto
3 Gerhard Berger
2 Riccardo Patrese

RACES CONTESTED

121 Alain Prost
99 Jackie Stewart
72 Jim Clark
171 Niki Lauda
51 Juan-Manuel Fangio
141 Nelson Piquet
66 Stirling Moss
126 Jack Brabham
144 Emerson Fittipaldi
176 Graham Hill
32 Alberto Ascari
104 Nigel Mansell
128 Mario Andretti
116 Alan Jones
146 Carlos Reutemann
92 James Hunt
123 Ronnie Peterson
112 Jody Scheckter

126 René Arnoux
62 Ayrton Senna
105 Michele Alboreto
52 Gerhard Berger
160 Riccardo Patrese

POLE POSITIONS

33 Jim Clark
28 Juan-Manuel Fangio
24 Niki Lauda
20 Nelson Piquet
18 Mario Andretti
18 René Arnoux
17 Jackie Stewart
16 Stirling Moss
16 Alain Prost
16 Ayrton Senna
14 Alberto Ascari
14 James Hunt
14 Ronnie Peterson
13 Jack Brabham
13 Graham Hill
13 Jacky Ickx
12 Nigel Mansell
10 Jochen Rindt

Others
3 Gerhard Berger
2 Michele Alboreto
2 Riccardo Patrese
1 Andrea De Cesaris

FASTEST LAPS

28 Jim Clark
25 Niki Lauda
23 Juan-Manuel Fangio
23 Nelson Piquet
20 Stirling Moss
20 Alain Prost
15 Clay Regazzoni
15 Jackie Stewart
14 Jacky Ickx
13 Alan Jones
12 René Arnoux
11 Alberto Ascari
11 John Surtees
10 Mario Andretti
10 Jack Brabham
10 Graham Hill

Others
9 Nigel Mansell
7 Ayrton Senna
5 Gerhard Berger
3 Michele Alboreto
3 Riccardo Patrese
2 Derek Warwick
1 Andrea De Cesaris
1 Teo Fabi

Foreword

Since I retired from actively driving in Grand Prix motor racing, I have visited many countries in my capacity as an 'expert commentator' with a variety of television networks.

At every event there is a battery of host commentators. Each network has its contracted specialist. Some are good, some excellent, some very effervescent, and of course some are simply not at all good! A great many become important in their own area of endeavour and even public figures, almost stars.

Murray Walker is truly exceptional. If I were asked today to choose someone with whom I would like to work on the telecast of a major motor racing event, I would choose Murray. There is no one who works harder, is more conscientious, or has available more research (done by himself) than any specialist journalist commentator I know. His command of the English language is indeed impressive, his choice of words colourful and descriptive, but above all the enthusiasm with which he energises the spirit of the event for his viewers on television has become a 'trademark'.

He has become a star in the United Kingdom, Canada, and most certainly in Australia. He is the friend of mechanics and team personnel, is respected and accepted by the drivers, and well recognised for his professional approach and execution, by cameramen, producers and directors. With Murray Walker there is no 'Take Nine' when doing an opening or introduction to a feature. When he does drop the ball, and it sometimes happens, his 'errors' become legend!

From the above remarks you will recognise that I like Murray Walker! I like what he does and how he does it, and I like him as a man! The image he projects is good and he has now carried the baton a stage further by being a writer. I very much enjoyed his last book on Grand Prix racing and this one is overflowing with facts, figures and 'Walkerisms'. There is a wonderful neutrality about his observations, and because he has been involved in all the events that he relates to, he has an authoritative view which I am sure you are going to enjoy.

Murray Walker is one of a kind. I am glad he has taken to writing as well as talking about Grand Prix motor racing. This way I can have his view on each event rather than just the rare occasions I am able to watch him on television.

JACKIE STEWART

The Drivers of 1988

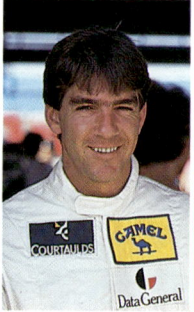

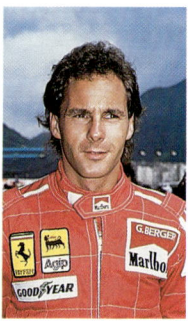

Michele Alboreto   Philippe Alliot   René Arnoux   Julian Bailey   Gerhard Berger

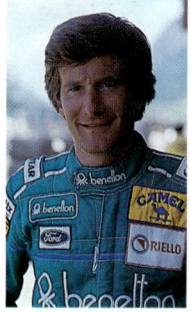

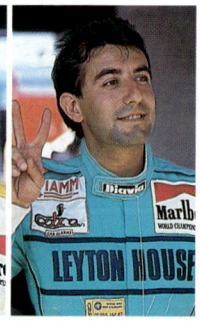

Thierry Boutsen   Martin Brundle   Alex Caffi   Adrian Campos   Ivan Capelli

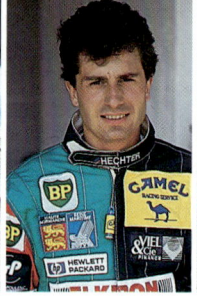

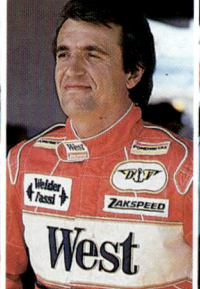

Eddie Cheever   Yannick Dalmas   Andrea De Cesaris   Piercarlo Ghinzani   Mauricio Gugelmin

Stefan Johansson	Nicola Larini	Oscar Larrauri	Nigel Mansell	Pierluigi Martini
Stefano Modena	Satoru Nakajima	Alessandro Nannini	Jonathan Palmer	Riccardo Patrese
Nelson Piquet	Alain Prost	Luis Perez Sala	Jean-Louis Schlesser	Bernd Schneider
Ayrton Senna	Philippe Streiff	Aguri Suzuki	Gabriele Tarquini	Derek Warwick

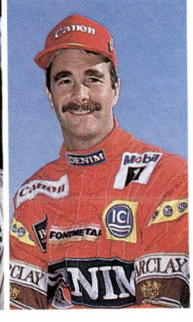

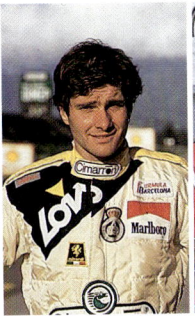

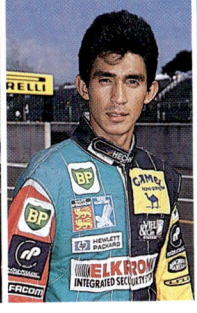

DRIVERS, TEAMS AND CARS — Declared at beginning of 1988 Formula One Season

No.	Name	Nationality	Age	No. GP's	No. Victories	Teams	Cars
1.	Nelson Piquet	BRA	35	141	20	Camel Lotus-Honda	100T
2.	Satoru Nakajima	JAP	35	16	—	Camel Lotus-Honda	100T
3.	Jonathan Palmer	GBR	31	54	—	Tyrrell-Ford	DG/017
4.	Julian Bailey	GBR	26	—	—	Tyrrell-Ford	DG/017
5.	Nigel Mansell	GBR	33	104	13	Canon Williams-Judd	FW12
6.	Riccardo Patrese	ITA	34	160	2	Canon Williams-Judd	FW12
9.	Piercarlo Ghinzani	ITA	36	65	—	West Zakspeed	881
10.	Bernd Schneider	GER	23	—	—	West Zakspeed	881
11.	Alain Prost	FRA	33	121	28	Marlboro McLaren-Honda	MP4/4
12.	Ayrton Senna	BRA	28	62	6	Marlboro McLaren-Honda	MP4/4
14.	Philippe Streiff	FRA	32	38	—	AGS-Ford	JH23
15.	Mauricio Gugelmin	BRA	24	—	—	Leyton House March-Judd	881
16.	Ivan Capelli	ITA	24	19	—	Leyton House March-Judd	881
17.	Derek Warwick	GBR	33	84	—	USF & G Arrows-Megatron	A10B
18.	Eddie Cheever	USA	30	87	—	USF & G Arrows-Megatron	A10B
19.	Alessandro Nannini	ITA	28	31	—	Benetton-Ford	B188
20.	Thierry Boutsen	BEL	30	73	—	Benetton-Ford	B188
21.	Nicola Larini	ITA	23	1	—	Stievani Osella-Alfa Romeo	FA1L
22.	Andrea De Cesaris	ITA	28	103	—	Rial-Ford	ARC1
23.	Adrian Campos	SPA	27	15	—	Lois Minardi-Ford	M188
24.	Luis Perez Sala	SPA	28	—	—	Lois Minardi-Ford	M188
25.	René Arnoux	FRA	39	126	7	Lotto Ligier-Judd	JS31
26.	Stefan Johansson	SWE	31	60	—	Lotto Ligier-Judd	JS31
27.	Michele Alboreto	ITA	31	90	5	Ferrari	F187
28.	Gerhard Berger	AUS	28	52	3	Ferrari	F187
29.	Yannick Dalmas	FRA	26	3	—	Larousse Calmels Lola-Ford	LC88
30.	Philippe Alliot	FRA	33	48	—	Larousse Calmels Lola-Ford	LC88
31.	Gabriele Tarquini	ITA	26	1	—	Coloni-Ford	FC188
32.	Oscar Larrauri	ARG	33	—	—	EuroBrun-Ford	188
33.	Stefano Modena	ITA	24	1	—	EuroBrun-Ford	188
36.	Alex Caffi	ITA	24	14	—	Scuderia Italia Dallara-Ford	F188

APPENDIX
During the course of the 1988 season, Pierluigi Martini (ITA) replaced Adrian Campos in the Minardi team, Martin Brundle (GBR) and Jean-Louis Schlesser (FRA) each drove on one occasion for Williams, the latter making his F1 debut. Aguri Suzuki (JPN) replaced Yannick Dalmas in the Lola for the Japanese Grand Prix. It was his first F1 race.

Preface

AS my British Airways Jumbo lifted off the ground at Adelaide the day after last year's Australian Grand Prix my feelings were mixed. Immense pleasure that another World Championship season had finished on such a high note but frustration that it was to be twenty weeks before the beginning of the next! Feelings, I'm sure, that were shared by everyone concerned with the exciting and dramatic world of Formula One.

Nothing stays the same in Grand Prix racing for long and 1988 was to see major changes which seemed likely to make a great spectacle even better. New rules that were designed to narrow the performance gap between the 1½ litre turbocars and their 3½ litre normally-aspirated rivals. New cars and engines, new drivers, new sponsors and, inevitably in a situation where there are now far more countries wanting to hold Grands Prix than there are dates available, revisions to the calendar and venues.

In the final year of turbocharged engines the teams using them faced some demanding regulations alterations. The maximum turbo boost, limited by 'pop-off' valves which open if the pressure exceeds the permitted limit, was to come down from 4.0 bar (four times normal atmospheric pressure) to 2.5 — a massive 37.5% reduction. Fuel allowance was to be reduced from 195 litres per race to 150 (23% less). The anticipated result was a power reduction from some 850 race horsepower in 1987 to some 650 in 1988. In comparison the 3½ litre cars, with the benefits of no fuel restriction and a lighter weight limit, were expected to produce about 620 horsepower. Testing during the winter suggested not only that the 2.5 bar turbocars were little slower than their 1987 predecessors but that they were also little faster than the 1988 'atmospherics' especially on the slower circuits. The deciding factors therefore, looked likely to be overall team efficiency, driver ability and fuel consumption — an intriguing prospect.

With thirty-one drivers registered to take part in races where the permitted maximum number of starters was twenty-six, it was strangely ruled that there would have to be pre-qualifying during the Friday morning practice periods to reduce to thirty the number taking part in the two qualifying sessions. And with a new safety rule requiring the drivers' feet to be behind the centre-line of the front wheels (except, as a special dispensation for 1988 only, for turbo teams using their 1987 chassis) virtually every team produced all-new cars including, in many cases, dramatically revised gearbox and fuel tank layouts designed to move weight forward in order to benefit handling.

The sixteen 1988 Grands Prix then were to see some major changes amongst the teams' cars. A new McLaren (MP4/4) designed by Steve Nichols and his team of technicians,

Alain Prost — a record 28 Grand Prix victories to his name. More in 1988?

9

with overall co-ordination by ex-Brabham designer Gordon Murray, with Honda engines instead of the Porsche-designed and built TAG V6s. Williams, Ligier and March cars powered by the new 3½ litre normally-aspirated British Judd V8 instead of their previous Honda and Megatron turbo and Ford DFZ atmospheric engines. Benetton with a much-revised four-valve Ford DFR 3½ litre motor in place of their former Ford V6 turbo. Osella with a revised 'Osella' engine based on their aged 1½ litre Alfa-Romeo turbo. Minardi with Ford DFZ atmospheric power in place of their failed Motori Moderni turbos. A new Lotus (their 100th Grand Prix design) without their innovative Active Suspension system which had proved to be too complicated, too heavy, too expensive, and too power-hungry. But, paradoxically, the new Williams cars were to have a revised version of their simpler active-suspension whilst other teams, notably Benetton, were working to perfect their versions of what appeared to be the thing to have. Ferrari, luxuriating in the situation of being able to use a developed version of their winning 1987 turbo car whilst being ready to move, when they felt the time was right, to an all-new John Barnard-designed car with semi-automatic transmission and an equally all-new 3½ litre V12 engine, the sound of which was something we all longed to hear!

Six turbo teams were to start the season (McLaren-Honda, Lotus-Honda, Ferrari, Arrows-Megatron, Zakspeed and Osella-Alfa) against twelve with normally-aspirated power. Williams, Ligier and March with Judd engines and the rest with various specifications of Ford power (where would Grand Prix racing be without Ford?) Five of them were familiar, namely, Benetton, Tyrrell, Lola, AGS and Minardi, but four were new or nearly so. The EuroBrun team, an offshoot of Swiss businessman Walter Brun's very successful sportscar racing organisation. RIAL, a new team founded by the mercurial German wheel magnate Gunther Schmidt. Team Italia, another new equipe using cars constructed by Dallara, and a re-emergence of the Coloni team which had appeared twice during the 1987 season. But, to everyone's enormous regret, 1988 was not to see any Brabham cars on the starting grids for the first time since the highly-respected team had made their Grand Prix debut in 1962. With two Constructors' Championships, four Drivers' Championships and 35 Grand prix victories behind them they were going to be very sadly missed but hopefully team boss Bernie Ecclestone would have over-

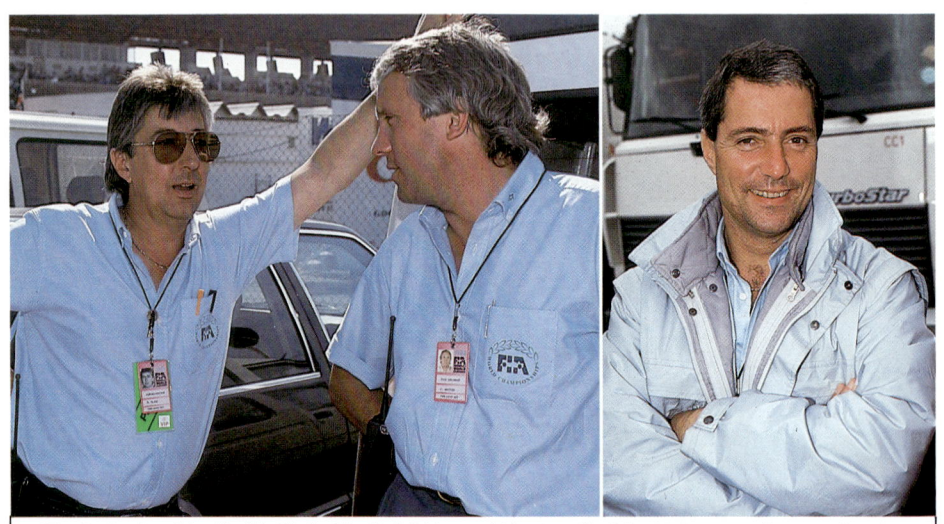

'The Professionals' — Herbie Blash, Charlie Whiting and Alan Woollard the FOCA team whose work makes everyone else's possible at all Grands Prix.

come engine availability and other problems in time to return the popular Brabham team to the Championship scene in 1989.

It never ceases to amaze me how much driver movement there is in Grand Prix racing every year. At the start of the 1988 season eighteen of the thirty-one registered drivers had switched teams or were new to Formula One — and they included some major changes. Ayrton Senna from Lotus to McLaren, for instance, to join the most successful Grand Prix driver of all time, Alain Prost — what a combination! World Champion Nelson Piquet from Williams to Lotus and Stefan Johansson from McLaren to Ligier. Other moves were Riccardo Patrese and Andrea de Cesaris from Brabham to, respectively, Williams and the new RIAL team. Alessandro Nannini from Minardi to Benetton. Piercarlo Ghinzani from Ligier to Zakspeed where he would be accompanied by newcomer Bernd Schneider the 1987 German Formula Three Champion. Mauricio Gugelmin, another Brazilian ace, was to make his move from Formula 3000 to Formula One by joining Ivan Capelli in the March team and Philippe Streiff had left Tyrrell to re-join AGS for whom he had previously driven in Formula Two and Formula 3000. Which left seven new, or almost new, comers to Grand Prix racing. Notably Stefano Modena the talented young ex-kart World Champion who had won the F3000 Championship in his first year in the category and who had had a single drive for Brabham in the 1987 Australian GP. Modena from Italy and Oscar Larrauri from Argentina were to drive the new EuroBrun car whilst Alex Caffi moved to the Dallara of Team Italia from Osella where he was replaced by Nicola Larini (ex Coloni 1987). In turn Larini's place in the Coloni car was to be taken by the Italian ex-Formula 3000 driver Gabriele Tarquini (who had driven an Osella in last year's San Marino GP). Frenchman Yannick Dalmas who had driven for the Lola team with great distinction in the last three races of '87 signed for a full 1988 season with the French team and Spaniard Luis Sala joined Minardi and fellow-countryman Adrian Campos. As is often the case veteran team owner Ken Tyrrell was the last to reveal his second driver and when he did it was to make the

Marlboro give an enormous amount to motor racing.

enormously welcome announcement that, by signing the gifted Julian Bailey to join Jonathan Palmer, 'atmospheric' World Champion in 1987, his team would have an all-British driver line-up, for the first time in it's 21-year-old history.

All of which meant that four men had disappeared from 1987's list of competitors — Martin Brundle who had sadly but very sensibly decided that winning World Championship Sportscar races with Jaguar was better than losing Grands Prix with Zakspeed, Teo Fabi who had left Benetton to race the new CART Porsche in America and, most regrettably, those very capable and likeable drivers Christian Danner and Roberto Moreno.

So, as we set off for Brazil for the first Grand Prix of the year (with the knowledge that Austria, unable to comply in time with FISA instructions to make essential safety-oriented changes to its magnificent Osterreichring, was to have its race replaced by a welcome return to Canada) the prospects were for a magnificent but unpredictable season of World Championship Grand Prix racing. On paper the three top teams had to be McLaren-Honda (Prost and Senna), Lotus-Honda (Piquet) and Ferrari (Alboreto and Berger). But very real challengers for the top honours had also to be Williams-Judd (Mansell and Patrese), Arrows-Megatron (Cheever and Warwick) and Benetton-Ford (Boutsen and Nannini). And, dependent on how their new 3½ litre cars went, 'dark horses' were Ligier-Judd (Arnoux and Johansson), March-Judd (Capelli and Gugelmin) and Tyrrell-Cosworth (Palmer).

The possibilities for drama, excitement and upsets seemed limitless. How would 'Superstars' Prost and Senna get on together in the same team? Would being Number One driver in his team for the first time in his long career really help Nigel Mansell? Would again receiving the preferential attention of his team (as he had for so long at Brabham) benefit Nelson Piquet practically and psychologically? Would Ferrari be able to repeat their 1987 end-of-season winning form? Would Alboreto be able to match Berger? Would the race performances of the experienced Arrows drivers, Cheever and Warwick, match their impressive testing achievements? Would the closer power, lighter weight and unlimited fuel of the top 3½ litre normally-aspirated teams (Williams, Tyrrell, Lola, Benetton, March and Ligier) enable them to beat the turbos and if so which would it be? Would we see any surprises from the 'triers' — Zakspeed, Osella, AGS, Minardi, RIAL, EuroBrun and Dallara and would the qualifying sessions be even more fraught than usual in a situation where an unusually high number of newcomers would be chasing their more experienced rivals in cars of similar potential performance. The season looked good and I awaited it with great anticipation.

Williams aerodynamicist Frank Dernie — a very talented man.

Doctors in the house — always wanted, hopefully never needed.

3rd April 1988
Circuit: Autodromo Nelson Piquet,
Rio de Janeiro

Brazil

BENEATH me, on the northerly flight-approach to Rio de Janeiro, is a seemingly never-ending horizon to horizon carpet of impenetrable-looking forest with not a dwelling in sight. Brazil is truly an enormous country! But eventually there's the awe-inspiring mountain-girdled descent to the city itself amidst bare rocky peaks jutting out of a solid ceiling of cloud — with a mounting feeling of excitement at the thought that here, on the newly named Autodromo Nelson Piquet, the questions we'd been asking all winter were about to be answered.

How would the lower-boost, reduced fuel allowance turbocars go against their lighter 3½ litre normally-aspirated rivals? With a dramatic reduction of the turbocars' power advantge over their 'atmospheric' competition how critical would fuel efficiency be? How would driver team-switches affect their competitiveness? Was a Grand Prix star going to emerge from the newcomers?

The winter tests had indicated that Ferrari had maintained their 1987 end of season edge over the competition, that the new McLaren looked like being another winner from Woking and that the FW12 Williams-Judd was right on the pace. But had the teams been sandbagging and how much were development problems of so many all-new cars going to affect the first race of the 1988 World Championship? It had been a long wait but on Sunday evening we would start to know!

Rio doesn't change. Same vibrant, sun-soaked atmosphere tinged with menace. Same exhaust-polluted traffic jams. Same unfinished seedy-looking buildings. Same glorious golden beaches with their seething crowds. Nor was it different at the flat and featureless circuit along the coast. Same super-abrasive surface (although Goodyear accurately forecast fewer tyre stops this year as a result of the reduced engine power). Same broiling heat — 104 degrees from ten in the morning until four in the afternoon on

Friday — and the same frenzied efforts by the local media to create a sensation. To his great discredit World Champion Nelson Piquet satisfied them and demeaned himself and the Sport on which he should reflect credit by publicly insulting Ayrton Senna and Nigel Mansell and his charming wife Rosanne.

But on Friday morning after McLaren's Gordon Murray had sagely said 'the talking is about to stop' it did just that — at ten o'clock as the 31 blaring, multi-coloured cars rolled out of their distinctively-roofed pit lane garages to open the 1988 season. Everyone expected turbocars to pack the top places on the starting grid but no one expected the sensational laps that Nigel

New boy with new team — Senna studies times with (L to R) Neil Oatley, Gordon Murray, Ron Dennis and Steve Nichols.

13

Easing his way back — Nigel Mansell's first race since Mexico '87 — and minus the moustache.

Mansell produced in the lesser-powered Williams-Judd. Fully fit after his practice crash in Japan five months earlier he rocketed round the Autodromo and, despite giving away some fifty horsepower to the Ferraris, the Lotus and the Honda-powered McLarens, took a superb second place on the grid — his sixteenth successive front row position. Second to Brazil's Ayrton Senna who, in his first race-meeting drive for McLaren, took his seventeenth pole position less than two seconds slower than Mansell's 1987 pole time (achieved with four-bar boost and at least 350 horsepower more). An outstanding and very significant achievement.

With Prost third on the grid ahead of Berger, Piquet and Alboreto there was only one normally-aspirated car — Mansell's — in the top six but with Boutsen's Benetton, Patrese's Williams and Capelli's March next up there were four in the top nine. Things looked interesting for Sunday! But already there was a feeling of *déjà vu* in the paddock for McLaren seemed to have done it again. Their all-new MP4/4 had only just been finished in time for the end of the Rio test two weeks before and both Senna and Prost were saying that it was far from right. But with Honda power and despite 'nervous' handling they were first and third fastest in practice! Was it going to be 1984 all over again, when between them Lauda and Prost won twelve of the sixteen Grands Prix?

On Sunday it certainly looked like it for the incomparable Alain Prost simply dominated the race, as he had in 1987 (also in a brand new car) to lead every one of the sixty laps and win his fifth Brazilian GP in seven years. But before his *tour de force* which won him his 29th World Championship race there had been totally unexpected drama. As pole-sitter Senna left the dummy grid to commence the parade lap — followed by the other 25 drivers — his gear selector mechanism broke, leaving him to crawl round jammed in first gear — to the vast discomfort of the overheating-prone Judd-powered and Benetton-Ford drivers. Amidst furious arm-waving the start was aborted and Senna leapt into the spare McLaren to start from the pit-lane — together with Capelli who had also had to change cars after his March-Judd blew a water hose on the grid.

So Mansell started from what was effectively pole position to be rapidly passed by the turbo-boosted Prost McLaren and Berger's Ferrari. But for eighteen glorious laps Nigel kept ahead of everyone else whilst worriedly watching his temperature gauge climbing to the danger zone. On lap nineteen it was all over. Into the pits to investigate. And there his engine not only stopped but refused to restart. But it had been a magnificent charge which showed not only that Mansell had lost none of his speed but that an 'atmospheric' car might be able to challenge the turbos in 1988.

With Prost watching his fuel gauge and pacing himself at the front Berger set about trying to catch him. But for the much smaller than usual Brazilian crowd — inflation is rampant and times are hard — there was only one man in the race — Senna. For with a truly memorable drive of pure brilliance

Race 1 — BRAZIL

Ayrton was making an incredible recovery. From his pit lane start he was 21st on lap one. Fifteenth on lap four. An astounding eighth on lap ten. In the points at sixth three laps later. Past Boutsen to fourth on lap eighteen and on lap twenty, following Mansell's retirement, he had disposed of Berger and was second! A drive that those who were privileged to see will never forget.

Prost made his sole stop for tyres on lap 26 without losing his lead (nearly everyone else stopped twice — another sign of the Frenchman's class) and on the next lap in came Senna for new boots — only to stall his engine. Out in sixth place to start all over again only to be shown the black flag, brought in and cruelly excluded for starting the race in his spare car after the parade lap. Justice? Well maybe but unpardonably long-delayed justice. For the second race in succession Senna had lost second place because of a technicality; Australia 1987 for extra brake ducting on his Lotus and now this. But his time would come.

The excitement was far from over though. Berger's determined efforts were yielding results. With a blistering charge which included a new lap record at 121.9 mph

Back to No. 1. World Champion Nelson Piquet in new colours.

15

TEAM ANALYSIS

LOTUS
As a result of being joined by World Champion Nelson Piquet Team Lotus proudly carry race numbers One and Two on new 100T cars. Second year with Honda turbocharged engine but 1987 'Active' suspension abandoned due to weight and power loss penalties. Piquet qualifies fifth after overcoming balance problems. Races to fast and reliable third place in car seemingly not yet a match for the major opposition. Nakajima benefitting from 1987 experience, starts from highest-ever tenth place. Like Piquet drives steady race to finish excellent sixth. Encouraging start for Lotus with five Constructors Championship points.

TYRRELL
Dismal and disquieting debut for new 017 car driven by Jonathan Palmer and GP newcomer Julian Bailey (first all-British driving team in Tyrrell 21 year history). Major handling deficiencies prevent Bailey from qualifying and limit Palmer to 22nd on grid (13th of twenty 'atmospheric' cars). Despite problems Palmer struggles to tenth before retiring, lap 48, with broken driveshaft. Back to the drawing board for designer Brian Lisles!

WILLIAMS
Superb new FW12 car with Judd 3½ litre V8 atmospheric engine and 'Reactive' suspension driven by now clean-shaven Nigel Mansell (officially designated Team Number One for the first time in 104 GP career) and Riccardo Patrese. Mansell a stunning second fastest in practice (sixteenth successive front row start). Brilliantly holds third place for 18 laps before retiring, lap 19, when overheated engine cannot be restarted after stalling during investigatory pit stop. Patrese qualifies eighth and retires from eighth on lap seven with too-hot Judd. Williams very much the class of the atmospheric teams, despite power deficiency, and clearly capable of challenging turbocars when engine cooling corrected.

ZAKSPEED
All the way from Niederzissen to Rio for nothing. New Zakspeed drivers, veteran Piercarlo Ghinzani and first-timer Bernd Schneider, both fail to qualify as a result of engine, electrical and circuit-ignorance (Schneider) problems. And to fill team's cup of misery new British race engineer Dave Kelly suffers heart attack.

McLAREN
Devastating debut for all-new, Honda powered, MP4/4 car — designed by Steven Nichols-led team and a crushing demonstration of the fact that there is life after John Barnard! Despite gearbox, nose mounting and car balance problems Prost qualifies third and dominates race to win 29th GP and fifth in Brazil in seven years — easily leading from first corner to finish with only one tyre stop. Team newcomer Ayrton Senna takes seventeenth pole position of career. Causes first start to be aborted when gear linkage breaks. Takes delayed start from pit lane in spare car. Brilliantly races from last to second place (lap 20). Stalls engine during lap 27 tyre stop. Rejoins sixth but belatedly black-flagged and excluded, lap 32, for infringing race-start rules. On Brazil form McLaren look set for both Driver and Constructor Championships.

'A word in your "shell-like" Alain' — Carlos Reutemann talks to 'Le Professeur'.

AGS
All-new car with Ford DFZ atmospheric engine for lanky ex-Tyrrell driver Philippe Streiff. Qualifies 19th (tenth NA). To seventeenth lap one but, hampered by brake problems, falls back before retiring from last place (15th: lap 36) as a result of harmlessly going off. Neat car shows great promise in comparison with lumbering 1987 device.

MARCH
Tremendously impressive all-new, superb looking, Adrian Newey-designed car for Ivan Capelli and GP debut of Brazilian Mauricio Gugelmin. Excellent qualification achievements — Capelli ninth and Gugelmin 13th. Gugelmin transmission fails at start. Capelli starts last from pit lane in spare car after blowing water hose on first parade lap. Improves to 17th, lap six, but retires, lap 17, with overheated Judd engine. Like Senna, technically disqualified for starting infringement. Early bath for all but obvious great potential for team once teething problems overcome.

ARROWS
Best Arrows race for long time. Ross Brawn-developed A10B version of 1987 car with Heini Mader/Megatron turbo engine benefiting greatly from reduced 2.5 bar boost. Pop-off valve problems in practice but Warwick

Race 1 — BRAZIL

qualifies eleventh and furious Cheever 15th after being fined $5,000 for alleged (and vigorously refuted!) safety infringement. Trouble free, typically determined, race drive to well merited fourth by Warwick ('as many points here as the whole of last season!'). Cheever drives to dogged eighth with stuck-open wastegate (pressure relief valve).

BENETTON
Yet another superb handling, all-new, car from Rory Byrne (his fourth in four years) with new V8 Ford DFR atmospheric engine. Newcomer Alessandro Nannini confirms outstanding talent with third fastest times during Friday and Sunday practice but qualifies twelfth due to Saturday problems. Seventh place laps one to six but retires lap seven with overheated engine. Another fine Boutsen race. From early sixth improves to excellent third and leading 'atmospheric', laps 42-45. Falls back with overheated engine to finish disappointed seventh (one lap down). But the promise is there ...

OSELLA
New driver, Nicola Larini, but same old car albeit with colourful new paint job and revised Osella internals for venerable Alfa-Romeo V8 turbomotor. Larini fails to qualify and looks forward to new chassis for next GP at Imola.

RIAL
Impressive debut for new German team formed by ex-ATS boss Gunther Schmidt with superb car drawn by ex-Ferrari designer Austrian Gustav Brunner, powered by atmospheric V8 Ford DFZ and driven by Andrea de Cesaris. Praiseworthy 14th (7th NA) on starting grid. De Cesaris drives mature race steadily improving to outstanding sixth (second NA) laps 21-25. Post tyre-stop brake and engine problems cause lap 54 retirement when ninth.

MINARDI
With relieved abandonment of the troublesome Motori Moderni turbo motor Giacomo Caliri produces a neat new car with well-proven V8 Ford DFZ, for Spaniards Adrian Campos and ex-F3000 racer Luis Perez-Sala. Sala qualifies 20th. Campos 23rd. Both retire with broken rear wing support when last but one — Campos on lap five (23rd) and Sala on lap 47 (11th).

LIGIER
After last year's catastrophe-on-wheels designer Michel Tetu breaks dramatic new ground for 1988. Modular construction with power steering and two fuel tanks sandwiching the Judd V8 atmospheric engine. At Rio the shapely but overweight result seems little better with massive oversteer and a flexible chassis. Arnoux starts 18th, progresses to 14th but retires from 16th (lap 23) when clutch disintegrates. Despondent Ligier recruit Stefan Johansson dispenses with power steering and wrestles to 21st on grid. After dropping to 24th in race, plugs on to last classified place, ninth, three laps down. Such a pretty car. Such a pity.

FERRARI
After 1987's triumphant double-victory finale and encouraging winter testing great expectations for developed but basically unchanged 187. But expectations unrealised. Amidst fractious and recriminatory team atmosphere Alboreto and Berger openly critical of lack of power caused by early-opening pop-off valves and wastegate problems. Berger qualifies fourth. Alboreto sixth. After racing with leaders Alboreto slides to eleventh before finishing an irritated and lacklustre fifth. Berger, second for most of race, chases Prost. Closes gap from 32 seconds to ten, including record lap (1 min 32.9 sec = 121.9 mph. Six-tenths faster than Piquet/Williams-Honda 1986 time using four-bar boost) before frustratedly settling for six points. Ferrari engine men must try harder for Imola home race.

LOLA
Ralph Bellamy produces heavily updated Lola with Ford DFZ power just in time for team's first Brazil race (not ready for '87 event). Lola twins of Phillipe Alliot and Yannick Dalmas qualify 16th and 17th and run together for 24 laps. Dalmas ninth, laps 27-30, but retires lap 33 when engine cuts out. Alliot also retires from ninth, lap 41, with broken engine mount.

COLONI
Ex F3000 and GP Osella driver Gabriele Tarquini replaces Nicola Larini in updated Ford DFZ powered car. Qualifies 25th after engine, electrical and tyre wear problems. Races at tail of field with under-revving engine and acute understeer. Retires from 14th (out of 15) lap 36 (broken rear hub bearing).

EUROBRUN
Successful Group C Sportscar entrant and driver, Swiss slot machine magnate Walter Brun, diversifies into Formula One with dumpy, Ford DFZ powered, car produced by Italian Paolo Pavanello's ex-GP Euroracing organisation. Oscar Larrauri qualifies last at 26th for first GP bedeviled by electrical problems which recur on parade lap to prevent start. Surprise recruit Stefano Modena qualifies wary 24th ('car is OK but I don't know the circuit') but runs last laps 6-20 before retiring, lap 21, when engine cuts out.

DALLARA
A messy Grand Prix introduction for the new Team Italia, obliged by the rules to take a 1987 Formula 3000 Dallara to Rio due to the non-completion of their 1988 car. Ex Osella driver Alex Caffi convincingly fails to qualify. Hasty Saturday return to Italy to ready new car for Imola after an expensive and fruitless trip.

> *Mansell on line — he retired. Nakajima off line — he finished sixth.*

17

(six-tenths of a second quicker than Piquet's four-bar boost Williams-Honda 1986 time) he had reduced the gap to Prost's McLaren from over thirty seconds to ten. But there it stayed. Gerhard could do no more 'with my underpowered car' and settled for second. Piquet meantime had been having a re-run of many of his 1987 races for Williams. Fast. Reliable. And in the points. In his first Lotus-Honda drive he was not quick enough to catch the McLaren or the Ferrari but was too fast for the rest. Third place. Four points. A nice little starter for his fourth World Championship. It seemed unlikely but stranger things had happened . . .

Behind the leaders, as is all too often the case in Formula One Grand Prix racing, reliability was conspicuous by its absence. Only five cars went the full sixty laps distance and only nine were classified as finishers. Seventeen retirements out of twenty-six starters! If equally high-tech Grand Prix motorcycles can race wheel-to-wheel and nearly all finish why can't the cars? Answers on a postcard to Jean-Marie Balestre please!

But hats off though to three fine drivers who didn't make the podium. To Derek Warwick who, after eleven retirements in 1987, finished a superb fighting fourth in his Arrows to score as many points as he had in the whole of the previous season! To Piquet's team mate, the steady Satoru Nakajima who, greatly benefiting from his 1987 experience, brought the second Lotus-Honda home in the points at sixth. And to the quiet and gifted Thierry Boutsen who deserved much more than his seventh, no-points, place. He fought every inch of the way and for a time held and looked likely to retain third place. But in the closing stages the heat of Brazil got to his Ford DFR engine — as it had to team-mate Nannini's and the Williams-Judds — and Thierry was obliged to back off.

So at Rio the turbos ruled but with Ferrari in desperate need of more power, Lotus seemingly not yet up to it, the rapid Judd-

Good start — poor finish. Patrese takes early sauna after starting eighth.

Race 1 — BRAZIL

Full support from Brazilian fan.

powered Williams and March cars with cooling problems — as had the Ford powered Benettons — and the rest either too slow or too fragile (or both) I can finish the story of Brazil '88 with exactly the same words that I used last year. 'McLaren quietly announced their intention to spend the next three weeks before the San Marino Grand Prix (four this time, actually) testing and developing their new car to make it really work — a depressing prospect for the other teams.' But, Grand Prix racing being what it is, one they'd energetically face with every intention of defeating the McLaren machine at Imola.

Victory number 29 for Prost and a triumphant debut for the McLaren.

BRAZIL GRAND PRIX

Winner: Alain Prost, McLaren-Honda MP4/4-03   *Fastest Lap:* Gerhard Berger, 121.943 mph

GRID POSITION		RESULTS			WORLD CHAMPIONSHIP			
No.	Driver	Pos.	Driver	Car	Drivers	Pts	Constructors	Pts
12	Senna	1	Prost	McLaren-Honda MP4/4-03	1. Prost	9	1. McLaren-Honda	9
5	Mansell	2	Berger	Ferrari F187/88C-104	2. Berger	6	2. Ferrari	8
11	Prost	3	Piquet	Lotus-Honda 100T/2	3. Piquet	4	3. Lotus-Honda	5
28	Berger	4	Warwick	Arrows-Megatron A10B/02	4. Warwick	3	4. Arrows-Megatron	3
1	Piquet	5	Alboreto	Ferrari F187/88C-103	5. Alboreto	2		
27	Alboreto	6	Nakajima	Lotus-Honda 100T/1	6. Nakajima	1		
20	Boutsen	7	Boutsen	Benetton-Ford B188-02				
6	Patrese	8	Cheever	Arrows-Megatron A10B/01				
16	Capelli	9	Johansson	Ligier-Judd JS31/03				
2	Nakajima							
17	Warwick							
19	Nannini							
15	Gugelmin							
22	De Cesaris							
18	Cheever							
30	Alliot							
29	Dalmas							
25	Arnoux							
14	Streiff							
24	Sala							
26	Johansson							
3	Palmer							
23	Campos							
33	Modena							
31	Tarquini							
32	Larrauri							

1st May 1988
Circuit: Imola near Bologna

San Marino

IF ever proof were needed that Italy is very special when it comes to motor racing it is provided by the 150 mile drive from Milan to Imola, scene of round two of the 1988 World Championship. Just a few miles from the airport is Arese the home of Alfa-Romeo who have produced so many superb Grand Prix cars such as the legendary P3, 8C and 158. The Austostrada from Piacenza to Bologna parallels a major section of the truly evocative 'round Italy' Mille Miglia sports car circuit now, sadly, no longer seriously used but rich with memories of heroic drives by men like Nuvolari, Varzi, Caracciola, Ascari, Fangio and Moss. It includes Modena, the home of Ferrari and just thirty miles from there Mantova the domicile of, to me, the greatest driver the world has ever seen — Tazio Nuvolari. And twenty miles from Imola the historic city of Bologna was the headquarters of Maserati who, like Alfa-Romeo and Ferrari, produced a string of impressive Grand Prix cars — notably the outstanding 250F.

So if motor racing really matters to you your senses are reeling by the time you arrive at the Autodromo Dino Ferrari!

At Imola this year Italy had only one question — were Ferrari, a disappointment in Brazil after their winning revival at the end of 1987, going to satisfy the fanatical 'Tifosi' with their first home win since Tambay's victory at Imola in 1983? And that was a good question because Imola's anti-clockwise 3.13 miles lap with its super-fast sections, its gradient, sweeping bends and tight chicanes is notoriously tough on fuel consumption especially, this year, for the turbocars with their reduced allowance of 150 litres. Fuel efficiency allied to the right balance of power and handling are therefore the keys to success. So maybe, here, an 'atmospheric' team, rather than Ferrari or the other turbo teams, would succeed?

But as they lined up on the grid on Sunday afternoon it looked more than unlikely. The four practice sessions on Friday and Saturday had seen mixed weather — wet on Friday, dry on Saturday. Wet or dry though McLaren had been in a class by themselves. After a month of painstaking development of the brand new Honda-powered MP4/4 which had won straight out of the box in Brazil,

In spite of spinning Julian Bailey qualified 21st for his first Grand Prix.

Prost and Senna were even more dominant than they had been in Rio. Prost was quickest on Friday with Senna second. On Saturday the positions were reversed with Senna taking the eighteenth pole of his career four-fifths of a second faster than Alain but a stupifying 3.3 seconds quicker than Nelson Piquet's Lotus-Honda in third place! With a performance gap like that and the clinically competent Japanese Honda technicians confident that 150 litres would last them the 60 laps/188 miles it looked as though we were going to have two races —

one for Prost and Senna and the other for the rest.

Which didn't necessarily mean to say that things were going to be dull. Because only a whisker over a second covered the next ten cars — and five of them were 3½ litre 'atmospherics' in a situation where, in qualifying, the odds had been heavily stacked against them. Piquet, third in his Lotus whose chassis was clearly not as efficient as the McLaren's at exploiting Honda's superb turbocharged engine, was less than a tenth of a second faster than an inspired Alessandro Nannini who was revelling in the razor-sharp handling of his Benetton-Ford. Then came Berger (Ferrari), Patrese (Williams), Cheever (Arrows), Boutsen (Benetton), Capelli (excellent in the new March-Judd) and Alboreto (Ferrari). So mega-gloom at Imola for the Tifosi with Ferrari languishing down at fifth and tenth. And Nigel Mansell the man who'd been on the front row for his last sixteen races? Down at eleventh after being unable to get himself and his car together.

And dull the San Marino Grand Prix most certainly was not! Sure enough it did turn out to be two races in one but both of them were compelling in their very different ways. With a faultless departure Senna shot away from the grid to lead from start to finish as his team mate Prost had done in Brazil. But with an engine prone to stall, Prost's start was as bad as Senna's had been good and from second at the green light he dropped to sixth at the end of lap one — four seconds behind Senna. With Piquet, Patrese, Nannini and Berger ahead of him he methodically set about picking them off to get to grips with Senna. Past Nannini on lap three. Berger on five. Patrese on six. And effortlessly past the similarly-powered Piquet on lap eight — by which time Senna was over eight seconds away. On lap fifteen the gap was down to 6.2 seconds but try as, he might Prost could reduce it no further. In fact with Senna knowing the situation through his car-to-pit radio he controlled the gap from the front keeping it, as he told me afterwards, 'from six to ten seconds according to the traffic.'

Berger drove his heart out for pole — but spun.

Race 2 — SAN MARINO

lap record with four-bar boost) and six points which not only maintained his World Championship lead but raised his career total to 421.5 and made him the highest achiever of all time. A great afternoon's work for both of them for it also increased McLaren's lead in the Constructors' Championship to a massive fourteen points after only two races.

Race one then was interesting. Race two, for third place, was rivetting! Once he'd been passed by Prost on lap eight World Champion Nelson Piquet held it for all the remaining 52 laps except one. But far from easily. For with a Lotus chassis that would not allow him to maximise the power of his Honda engine as would the McLarens of Senna and Prost he was not only consistently some three seconds a lap slower than the two men ahead but was no quicker than the traffic jam behind him — composed, in varying order, of Patrese, Nannini, Berger, Boutsen and Mansell. For once Patrese had closed with him time and time again it was only Nelson's ability instantly to increase his power by pressing his 'extra boost' button that enabled him to stay ahead. And in doing that he so cut into his fuel that he had to regulate his pace according to his consumption gauge and only just made it to the finish — lapped by both the McLarens.

In a race of outstanding drives four men were, for me, especially impressive. Senna and Prost, of course, but also Nannini and Mansell — with Boutsen and Patrese almost as praiseworthy. Alessandro Nannini was superb and more than proved how right Benetton team boss Peter Collins had been to sign him. With turbo power Berger and Prost passed him on lap three but four laps later he was ahead of the Ferrari to close on and harry Patrese for a fourth place that the Williams driver stubbornly refused to yield with driving tactics that, at times, verged on the unacceptable. But on lap 25 Nannini took him to draw away and start an equally enthralling fight for third with Piquet which lasted for eleven unforgettable laps and which eventually led to his undoing — after consistently closing on the corners only to have to give best to Piquet's superior power on the straights and after literally getting his wheels between those of the Lotus —

Inspired Nannini caught Patrese — only to spin — before wheel-banging with Piquet.

With a 'slow' last lap he let it drop to 2.3 seconds as he crossed the line brilliantly to win his seventh Grand Prix and his first for McLaren. But Prost, in his pragmatic way, was well satisfied with second place, the fastest lap in one minute 29.685 seconds (less than a second slower than Piquet's 1986

TEAM ANALYSIS

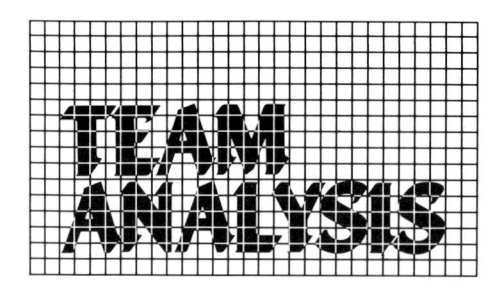

LOTUS
Post Brazil wind tunnel and Monza testing improves car for San Marino. New undertray and wings, suspension modifications and revised Honda throttle position to overcome premature opening of pop-off valve. Piquet unimpressive third on grid over three seconds slower than Senna's pole time and under one-tenth second faster than quickest NA car (Nannini's Benetton). After running second for seven laps, Piquet just holds third place whilst coping with race-long fuel consumption problem in effort to keep ahead of four Benetton and Williams drivers. Remains third in Drivers World Championship. Nakajima qualifies twelfth and finishes eighth, one lap down, also with consumption problems, dropping one place to seventh in Championship. Reliable Lotus retains third place in Constructors Championship.

TYRRELL
Major changes to car since Brazil in effort to improve handling — notably beefed-up suspension. Only partially successful. '25% better when needs to be 100%' says Jonathan Palmer who qualifies 23rd and finishes 14th (two laps down) with over-running engine. Julian Bailey does very well to qualify 21st for his first GP. To pit, lap eight, when 19th to tighten loose wheel. Recovers to 18th by lap 43 but retires, lap 49, with gear selector problems.

WILLIAMS
Williams spend post-Brazil four week gap developing new car. Revisions to NA Judd engine lubrication system to eliminate oil surge and work on Reactive suspension system. But 'still not getting best out of car.' With no real problems Mansell qualifies eleventh (first time for 17 races not on front row). Then drives magnificent fighting race. Gains five places by lap 26. Brilliantly passes Boutsen, Nannini and Piquet to third only to retire from fourth, lap 43, with electrical failure. Patrese qualifies well at sixth. With superb start holds third lap one to five. Then fourth until lap 24 before sliding down to finish 13th, two laps down, with cracked exhaust. 1987 Constructors' Championship winning team yet to score a point.

ZAKSPEED
Another awful weekend. Ghinzani qualifies 25th with wastegate problems. Trails at rear of field until lap 17 when retires short of two gears. Schneider again fails to qualify due to combination of pop-off valve problems and lack of circuit experience.

McLAREN
Second devastating 1988 demonstration of overwhelming McLaren-Honda superiority in terms of driver/engine/chassis combination. Senna and Prost take first two places on grid demoralisingly faster than Piquet at third. Senna's 18th pole position. With brilliant start Senna controls race from front to win his seventh GP and first for McLaren. Prost, after bad start, recovers from sixth, lap one, to finish excellent second with fastest lap (lap 53: one minute 29.68 seconds = 125.723 mph) less than a second slower than Piquet 1986 lap record. Both Senna and Prost lap everybody else. With 421.5 Championship points Prost becomes top scorer of all time. Prost and Senna now first and second in Drivers' Championship and dominating lead of 14 points in Constructors' Championship.

AGS
A most heartening meeting for the enthusiastic little French team gains new-found respect. Despite no winter testing at Imola Streiff achieves excellent car balance to qualify 13th (first time for AGS on top half of grid). Finishes encouraging tenth (two laps down) despite intermittent engine cut-out problem.

The FIA's intended performance-leveller — a pop-off valve.

MARCH
Post-Brazil development reduces car weight, improves suspension and aerodynamics and revises Judd NA engine lubrication system. After qualifying 20th Gugelmin races in mid-field to achieve first GP finish in 15th place (two laps down) with engine temperature, fuel consumption and gearbox problems. Capelli an excellent ninth on grid. Improves to eighth, lap two, but disappointingly retires lap three with broken gearbox.

ARROWS
Excellent work by Gerhard Schuman overcomes four-cylinder Megatron engine pop-off valve premature opening problem. Cheever a worthy seventh on grid and races strongly to finish seventh (one lap down). Warwick experiences handling and balance problems in practice. Qualifies 14th in spare car, but finishes ninth (two laps down). Both cars marginal on fuel at especially demanding Imola.

BENETTON
With the exception of McLaren Benetton undoubtedly the class of the field at Imola. With superb-handling chassis and

24

Race 2 — SAN MARINO

Sala gave Minardi their best-ever GP result — 11th.

further improved Ford DFR engine a euphoric Alessandro Nannini qualifies magnificent fourth behind Honda-powered Senna, Prost and Piquet. In superb race drive fights up to fourth harrying Piquet for third before spinning down to seventh, lap 36. Audacious last lap 'off course' manoeuvre by Berger takes fifth place from Nannini who, despite sore foot and cracked exhaust, nevertheless gains first World Championship point (one lap down) together with fastest NA lap (lap 57: one minute 32.034 seconds). Boutsen, troubled by binding brakes plus engine and transmission problems, qualifies eighth but finishes top 3½ litre after fighting up to excellent fourth (one lap down) slowed by loss of power through cracked exhaust. Now fifth in Drivers' Championship.

OSELLA
Re-positioning of engine mounts on 1987 car results in it being deemed a 'new' car at scrutineering as a result of which the existing foot box design fails to meet revised 1988 construction regulations. Single Osella therefore disastrously excluded from the impecunious little Italian team's most important race. So no start for Nicola Larini.

RIAL
Two cars for Andrea de Cesaris one of which he destroys in first practice. Seizes differential in hastily finished second car but despite limited running qualifies well at sixteenth. Starts from pit lane after front left suspension pick-up pulls out of tub during Sunday warm up. Retires at end first lap.

MINARDI
Luxuriating in new-found reliability thanks to Ford DFZ power Spaniards Campos and Sala qualify 22nd and an encouraging 18th. Both race and finish well. Sala eleventh (two laps down) with 'no problems' and Campos 16th (three laps down) — his first ever finish in 17 Grands Prix. A heartening meeting for Minardi.

LIGIER
From bad in Brazil to worse in Imola. Despite a redesigned rear suspension the innovative new car remains totally inadequate in the grip and handling departments. This had nothing to do with Arnoux punting Prost off the track on Friday! Drastic experimentation with alternative suspension set-ups for Arnoux and Johansson fails to enable either to qualify — the first time ever for the French team who despondently return to Vichy to look for wind-tunnel solution.

FERRARI
Another dismal story. Work by Ferrari engine men fails to find enough power to depress the top normally-aspirated runners, and those with turbocharged Honda engines. A dispirited and out-psyched-by-Berger Alboreto qualifies tenth after wastegate problems. Berger fifth on grid but unhappy with car and over 3½ seconds off the pace. Alboreto 23rd on lap one after appalling start (clutch) fights up to eighth (lapped) on lap 43 but retires, lap 55, with blown motor. Berger to fourth lap three but, demeaningly passed by four NA cars, down to eighth laps 20 to 42. Eventually finishes unimpressive fifth after cutting corner to pass Nannini on last lap. Berger third in Drivers' Championship and Ferrari poor second in Constructors' contest.

LOLA
With unexpected and regretted departure of popular Australian designer Ralph Bellamy Lola boss Eric Broadley takes over development responsibility. Revised front suspension and nose since Rio. After qualifying 19th Dalmas drives steady race to finish 12th (two laps down) with 'no grip'. Alliot starts 15th and, similarly afflicted, finishes 17th (three laps down) having spent time at pit remedying suspension problem.

COLONI
Gabriele Tarquini, with previous experience of Imola, qualifies 17th. Gains four places on lap one but drops back to 14th, laps 11-39, before retiring from 18th, lap 41, with broken throttle linkage.

A hold-up! But scrutineers approve Modena's weight.

EUROBRUN
Driving the tubby Swiss-entered, Italian-built and Ford-powered cars Larrauri and Modena fail to impress. Larrauri non-qualifies. Modena, last on the grid at 26th, races last after early pit stop with damaged nose until retiring, lap 53, with malfunctioning gearbox.

DALLARA
Debut of well constructed, hump-backed, Sergio Rhinland-designed 1988 car with 3½ litre Ford DFZ power. Team not unhappy with Alex Caffi's 24th place on grid. Caffi improves to 20th, laps 8-17, but after losing power with broken exhaust, retires, lap 19, with gear selector breakage.

Superb Senna — pole position and first all the way.

Alessandro spun down to seventh. With the fastest atmospheric lap of the day (one minute 32.034 seconds which was beaten only by the five turbo cars of Senna, Prost, Berger, Cheever and Alboreto) he later got up to fifth only to lose it on the very last lap when Berger audaciously drove across him on the grass at the Aqua Minerale chicane. But Alessandro had made his point!

Nigel Mansell's was no less a drive. Having got the balance of his Williams-Judd to his satisfaction in the final Sunday half-hour practice (a superb third fastest) he gave a Prost-like vintage performance from his eleventh place start. Tenth on lap one. Ninth on three. Eighth on ten. Past Berger's Ferrari to seventh. Then Patrese's ailing Williams and into the points at sixth on lap 26. Remorselessly he closed on Boutsen and Nannini's Benettons. Past them and up to Piquet. And, stupifyingly, past the Lotus-Honda to third on lap 40! But once again Piquet's boost button regained him the place and three laps later Nigel was out (faulty voltge regulator/flat battery and, therefore, collapsed Reactive suspension). After just the sort of drive we've come to expect from him. No points after two races — a more than poor reward for magnificent drives in Brazil and Italy.

With Boutsen's gritty drive from eighth to fourth, taking Capelli, Cheever, Berger, Patrese and benefiting from Mansell's retirement on the way he, like Nannini,

Race 2 — SAN MARINO

showed that Benetton was a force to be reckoned with in 1988. And in the same way Patrese demonstrated that if Williams could overcome their various problems like his cracked exhaust and Mansell's electrics (a 'Judd' problem which also affected the March and Ligier cars) the Williams team would be there too. Both Arrows finished although they can't have been too happy at being convincingly outraced by so many atmospheric cars. But Ferrari? With Berger a lucky fifth and Alboreto retiring from eighth there was a lot to do before Monaco — and only two weeks to do it. Why should they be different though? Everyone else except McLaren had the same problem!

Everything looks good at March! Happiness for Mauricio Gugelmin — his first GP finish.

Some of the racing was close.

SAN MARINO GRAND PRIX

Winner: Ayrton Senna, McLaren-Honda MP4/4-01 **Fastest Lap:** Alain Prost, 125.723 mph

GRID POSITION		RESULTS		WORLD CHAMPIONSHIP			
No. Driver	Pos. Driver	Car		Drivers	Pts	Constructors	Pts
12 Senna	1 Senna	McLaren-Honda MP4/4-01		1. Prost	15	1. McLaren-Honda	24
11 Prost	2 Prost	McLaren-Honda MP4/4-04		2. Senna	9	2. Ferrari	10
1 Piquet	3 Piquet	Lotus-Honda 100T/2		3. Berger	8	3. Lotus-Honda	9
19 Nannini	4 Boutsen	Benetton-Ford B188-04		Piquet	8	4. Benetton-Ford	4
28 Berger	5 Berger	Ferrari F187/88C-104		5. Boutsen	3	=5. Arrows-Megatron	3
6 Patrese	6 Nannini	Benetton-Ford B188-03		Warwick	3		
18 Cheever	7 Cheever	Arrows-Megatron A10B/01		7. Alboreto	2		
20 Boutsen	8 Nakajima	Lotus-Honda 100T/1		8. Nakajima	1		
16 Capelli	9 Warwick	Arrows-Megatron A10B/02		Nannini	1		
27 Alboreto	10 Streiff	AGS-Cosworth JS23/1					
5 Mansell	11 Sala	Mindardi-Cosworth M188-03					
2 Nakajima	12 Dalmas	Lola-Cosworth LC88-02					
14 Streiff	13 Patrese	Williams-Judd FW12/2					
17 Warwick	14 Palmer	Tyrrell-Cosworth DG/017-1					
30 Alliot	15 Gugelmin	March-Judd 881/2					
22 De Cesaris	16 Campos	Minardi-Cosworth M188-01					
31 Tarquini	17 Alliot	Lola-Cosworth LC88-01					
24 Sala							
29 Dalmas							
15 Gugelmin							
4 Bailey							
23 Campos							
3 Palmer							
36 Caffi							
9 Ghinzani							
33 Modena							

15th May 1988
Circuit: Monte Carlo

Monaco

MONACO was to be the third of the Championship's varying types of circuit. Brazil's Autodromo Nelson Piquet is flat and featureless with a near-200 mph straight and a super-abrasive surface. Imola, with a bit of everything, makes special demands on fuel efficiency. But now came the very different Monaco which picturesquely threads its way up, down and twistingly round the streets of the mega-rich little Principality. A unique circuit where, because of its comparative slowness, fuel consumption is no problem but where dedication, stamina and the ability to drive a millimetre-perfect race for nearly two concentration-sapping hours most certainly is.

'Surely this is the place where someone will be able to beat McLaren?' people said uneasily as if to hearten themselves. For after two crushing demonstrations of overall superiority in Brazil and at Imola the 'Woking Wizards' had badly rattled the opposition. The McLaren MP4/4 chassis was clearly something very special indeed. Honda, in the words of Ferrari's Harvey Postlethwaite, had created an entirely new dimension in Grand Prix engine technology. Prost and Senna (who, between them, had won the last four Monaco Grands Prix) were supreme masters of their demanding craft and the amalgam of those three elements made a seemingly unbeatable combination.

Practice did nothing to dispel the prophesy that McLaren could win not only the Monaco GP but all sixteen rounds of the 1988 World Championship. Senna, leaving no team or personal stone unturned in his usual remorseless demand for absolute perfection of man and machine, took his third successive pole position of the season at 88.6 mph — an inhuman 1.4 seconds faster than his distinguished team-mate Alain Prost. One and a half seconds! At Monaco that is light years, and even though Ferrari had greatly improved their act with an all-red Berger/Alboreto second row it was a row that was over two and a half seconds slower than Senna. 2½ seconds times 78 laps equals well over three minutes. Or, put another way, nearly 2½ laps! That was what looked like being the magnitude of McLaren's potential dominance over the best of the rest, let alone the other slower 22 cars and drivers opposing them.

But even though the fastest of the lighter and allegedly nimbler 3½ litre cars, Mansell's Williams-Judd in a superb fifth place ahead of the turbocharged Lotus-Hondas and Arrows-Megatrons, was more than 3½ seconds off Senna's searing practice pace maybe, in some undefined way, the

Ayrton — a hint of a smile. Not later.

29

normally-aspirated clan would get the job done? But it hardly seemed likely. And they didn't.

At Monaco being on the front row with a clear road ahead is all. It is where seven winners in the last ten years had come from. And Senna and Prost were there. But with very different attitudes. Prost had won Monaco three times in the last four years. Senna had won there once — last year in the Lotus. Prost had absolutely nothing to prove but Senna had been trying to gain psychological superiority over the little Frenchman ever since the beginning of the season. Now the debriefing sessions after practice took four hours because of Senna's insistence on dissecting every nuance of what had happened. Senna had taken every pole position this year and he desperately wanted to make it two in a row at Monaco the most prestigious Grand Prix of them all. In short he was hungry to prove that he was Number One. Prost didn't have to. He was.

But when the lights turned to green the Brazilian's campaign seemed to be succeeding. With an absolutely superb getaway he led the colourful writhing snake of cars into St Devote where so many drivers' hopes have come to an impactful finish on the first lap. Which was exactly what happened to Alex Caffi's as Ivan Capelli crowded him into the barrier. But even earlier than that Philippe Streiff, after qualifying an excellent twelfth in the new AGS, had to draw into his pit and out of the race when his accelerator cable broke on the parade lap. Lap one saw the beginning and end of Nelson Piquet's race too. From his unimpressive eleventh place on the grid he had his nosecone rudely trodden on by Eddie Cheever's Arrows and had to retire when it was found to be impossible to fit a replacement. The Lotus cup of misery was thus full to the brim. Nakajima non-qualifying and the World Champion out with

Andrea De Cesaris — without a car again.

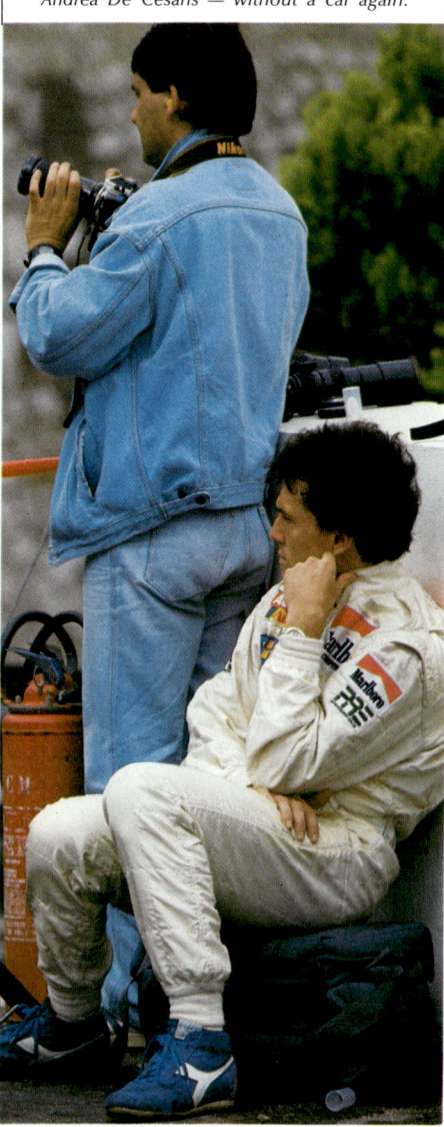

Wet practice for Prost but an easy race win — his fourth in five years at Monaco.

30

Race 3 —MONACO

Michele Alboreto — the Ferrari is beautiful but not a winner.

not a lap completed. Not at all what they needed after critical comments about their inability to make as good use of their Honda power as the all-conquering McLaren team.

Meanwhile up at the front Senna was scorching away from Berger who had passed Prost at the start when Alain missed his change to second gear. At the end of the Lap Ayrton led by a massive 2½ seconds from Berger, Prost, Nigel Mansell (who had taken Alboreto's Ferrari when Michele was baulked by the slow-starting Prost), Alboreto, Nannini, Patrese, Warwick and a brilliant Jonathan Palmer. And that's the way it stayed for the next 31 laps! Sounds dull but all the time Prost was glued to the gearbox of Berger's Ferrari and trying every way he knew to get past. But it was a different Gerhard from the one that Alain had psyched into spinning out of contention at Portugal in 1987 and he grimly stuck to his line. As did the inspired Nigel Mansell in fourth place ahead of Alboreto. But as his Judd engine was still liable to overheat, Nigel had to back off occasionally from shadowing Berger and Prost, to increase the air flow through his radiators. As he did so on lap 33 Alboreto tried an impossible passing manoeuvre at the swimming pool — and took Mansell off. A tragic end to a fine

Berger leading Prost — absorbing for 53 laps.

TEAM ANALYSIS

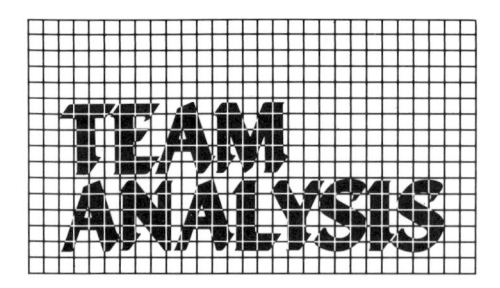

LOTUS
Ghastly Riviera weekend for Lotus. Despite post-Imola testing at Nogaro both drivers, each expressing strong dislike of Monaco, founder in practice. Nakajima fails to qualify for first time in GP career. Piquet, only eleventh on grid, retires at end of first lap after Lotus nosecone run over and mounting points destroyed. Drops to fourth in Championship. Lotus remain poor third in Constructors' Championship amidst adverse comment at their failure to match McLaren's effective use of Honda power.

Lotus disaster — Nakajima didn't qualify and Piquet was out on lap one.

TYRRELL
Glory for Palmer. Misery for Bailey. Relief and joy for Tyrrell. Jonathan Palmer, at circuit he loves, drives superbly in long wheelbase car in both practice and race. Personal best-ever tenth place on grid followed by inspired repetition of 1987 class-winning fifth place (one lap down with badly blistered hands) after race-long duel with Derek Warwick. Julian Bailey in less suitable short wheelbase car fails to qualify. Two invaluable points for Palmer and Tyrrell in their respective Championships.

WILLIAMS
Heartening improvement after Nogaro testing pinpoints previous electrical problems and improves engine cooling. Monaco-lover Nigel Mansell fifth on grid beaten only by turbo McLarens and Ferraris. Races at top of form. Strong, confident and very impressive fourth behind Senna, Berger and Prost until punted into retirement by contrite Alboreto, lap 33. Sadly still no points after three races. Patrese similarly impressive. Eighth on grid and sixth in race (one lap down) to score first Williams 1988 point despite pit stop to replace nosecone and punctured tyre after hitting off-line Alliot, lap 51. Outlook getting brighter at Didcot.

ZAKSPEED
Lacklustre Monaco outing. Unfortunate Bernd Schneider fails to qualify after adequate Friday time disallowed due to infringement of technical rules (air duct marginally oversize). Prevented from making first GP appearance by engine problem and going off on Saturday. Ghinzani starts 23rd, improves with retirements to 12th by lap 39 but retires lap 44 (gearbox).

McLAREN
Overall team superiority more than maintained at street circuit Monaco. Senna takes third successive 1988 pole position stunning 1.4 seconds quicker than next fastest Alain Prost. Leads from start to build dominating 55 second cushion. After running third for 53 laps Prost gets past Berger. Despite seemingly unassailable lead 1987 winner Senna, fearful of Prost threat, speeds up, makes fastest lap at one minute 26.321 seconds (86.24 mph) but loses concentration and hits barrier at Portier lap 67. Retires and drops to third in Championship. Fourth Monaco victory in five years increases Prost Championship lead over strongest rival (Senna) to commanding fifteen points. Even after Senna failure to score McLaren now lead Constructors' Championship by daunting thirteen points.

AGS
Getting better all the time — helped by strong budget from Channel Tunnel Bouygues construction company. After wind tunnel work at St Cyr car further improved by designer Christian Van der Pleyn. With spare car as back up for first time Philippe Streiff achieves best-ever grid position at twelfth. But no reward for praiseworthy achievement when accelerator cable breaks on assembly lap forcing instant retirement.

MARCH
After handling, grip and engine-related problems Gugelmin (first time at Monaco) and Capelli qualify 14th and 22nd. Gugelmin gradually improves to tenth at rear of remaining field, laps 41-45, before retiring, lap 46, (sheared fuel pump drive). Capelli hits Caffi after start and stops for repairs to suspension damage. Rejoins to run at rear of field, improving with retirements, to finish tenth (six laps down) in state of collapse with numb legs caused by confined cockpit. Gugelmin also unhappy with lack of room in aerodynamic-conscious Adrian Newey design.

ARROWS
Another excellent showing by revitalised long established team. Derek Warwick qualifies excellent seventh and races strongly and reliably to even better fourth (one lap down) despite 'boredom(!) and no brakes towards the end.' Retains Championship fifth place. Cheever qualifies ninth but retires lap nine with engine electrical pick-up problem. Team improve to fourth in Constructors' Championship.

Race 3 — MONACO

BENETTON
A disappointing meeting for the Witney team. Nannini continues excellent Imola form with strong sixth place on grid. Improves to fifth after Mansell retirement but out lap 39 when gearbox jams in sixth. Boutsen qualifies sixteenth after front wheel bearing, brake and power deficiency problems. Lack of car balance and lap 55 puncture limit recovery to eighth place (two laps down). Boutsen and Team strongly lead 3½ litre 'atmospheric' contest.

OSELLA
After catastrophe at Imola satisfaction at Monaco. Designer Antonio Tomaini revamps car to legal 'updated 1987' specification. Larini qualifies a worthy 25th and races reliably to ninth place (three laps down) at tail of field — achieving one of very few Osella finishes in the marque's history.

RIAL
Life is never dull with Gunther Schmid and Andrea de Cesaris! Talented designer Gustav Brunner, after inevitable row with team owner Schmid, allegedly Zakspeed-bound. De Cesaris writes off second RIAL in two meetings by ramming Berger's Ferrari in the tunnel and later has battery changed on-course for which offences fined total of $20,000 by FISA. Nevertheless qualifies 19th. Improves to 15th laps 1-3 and then to 11th, laps 18-28 before retiring, lap 29, with 'Clutch, gearbox and engine problems.'

MINARDI
A miserable Monaco after astounding revelation that the Minardi aerodynamics had been developed underwater in Sweden. Campos fails to qualify after hitting Jonathan Palmer Tyrrell and damaging car. In first Monaco GP appearance Sala justifiably happy with qualification at 15th. Improves to tenth by lap 33 but retires, lap 37, with breakage of both drive shafts (faulty batch).

René Arnoux — not in anyone's way!

LIGIER
Monaco little better than Imola for Guy Ligier's French team amidst general pit-lane agreement that new car unnecessarily complicated. After hitting guard rail twice Johansson just qualifies at 26th but retires from race, lap seven, with electrical problem and blown head gasket. Arnoux qualifies 20th but starts from pit lane in spare after

'Bored' Derek Warwick on his way to fourth and more Arrows points.

race car stops (electrics) on assembly lap. Races twentieth and last laps 10-17 before retiring lap 18 (electrics again). Crisis time at Vichy . . .

FERRARI
Impressive first and second places for Maranello — in the 'Non-McLaren' race! Post-Imola work on engine effects some improvement but still way behind Honda. Berger and Alboreto third and fourth on grid but some three seconds slower than Senna. Berger holds determined second just ahead of Prost for 53 laps. Passed on lap 54 but regains second and stays there when Senna retires lap 67. Moves ahead of Senna to second in Championship. Alboreto fights for fourth with Mansell for 32 laps and takes it by over-zealous passing manoeuvre which puts Nigel off (for which Gentleman Michele later apologises). Finishes third as result of Senna retirement. Ferrari, still in second place, slightly narrow Constructors' Championship gap to McLaren to 13 points.

LOLA
Following suspension modifications after Croix en Ternois testing Dalmas, Monaco F3 race winner in 1986, qualifies 21st and races impressively to finish excellent seventh after losing sixth place to charging Patrese on last lap. Alliot starts 13th and improves to ninth, laps 41-50, before baulking Patrese effort to lap him on approach to Mirabeau. Resultant major collision ends with happily uninjured Alliot in tyre wall with destroyed car.

COLONI
First time at Monaco for Tarquini. Qualifies 24th. Works way up to 18th laps 3-5 but retires lap six with broken rear suspension.

EUROBRUN
Another team with unhappy Monaco memories. Stefano Modena excluded after first practice for ignoring pits-entry signal to stop for car weighing. Oscar Larrauri starts 18th in first GP and stays there until lap 14 when retires after going off at Loews because 'I have a brake problem.'

DALLARA
Bad luck at Monaco for pleasant and hard-trying team. Alex Caffi qualifies commendable 17th but fails even to get round first corner when bundled into the barrier at St Devote immediately after start.

33

MURRAY WALKER'S GRAND PRIX YEAR

Hard work for Monaco spectators.

Race 3 — MONACO

Gerhard spins in front of the Coloni in practice. In the race he came second.

drive which would surely have seen Nigel in the points for the first time this year. Michele later humbly apologised for his misjudgement but the damage was done.

On lap 54 Alain Prost at last wore Berger down and got through to second — some fifty seconds behind Senna. Which you would have thought was more than enough for the Brazilian. But this was where 'Prost Power' took over. Uneasy in the knowledge that it was his strongest rival behind him Senna started swopping fastest laps with Prost until he was reassured on the radio by Team Manager Ron Dennis that his first place was not going to be challenged. Alain

Jonathan Palmer loves Monaco — in the points again.

was prepared to settle for second place and the six points that went with it. So Senna slowed down, lost concentration on lap 67 and spun off into the barrier at the Portier! An amazing thing for the experienced Brazilian to do. It was later suggested that he had had a slow puncture later denied by Senna. However, the race was lost for him and won, for the fourth time in five years, for Prost. A tribute both to his driving ability and his tactical prowess.

But all the action at Monaco wasn't up at the front. Derek Warwick drove a fine race to take his second fourth place of the season in his Arrows-Megatron. For all of his 77 laps he was fiercely chased by an absolutely inspired Jonathan Palmer who, for the second year in succession, took fifth place to win the 3½ litre class and two vital points for his team in a Tyrrell which was far from ideal for the twists and turns of Monaco — as Jonathan's badly blistered hands showed. The Williams team took their first 1988 point too — thanks to an excellent drive by Riccardo Patrese who finished sixth after a do-or-die effort on the last lap which demoted the excellent Yannick Dalmas's Lola. A stimulating race for Riccardo for he had a violent coming-together with the Lola of Philippe Alliot which chopped him off a the Mirabeau on lap 51 and went on into the barrier to destroy itself (with no harm to Alliot — except injured pride).

35

MURRAY WALKER'S GRAND PRIX YEAR

Mansell — no Monaco luck again — he was clouted by apologetic Alboreto.

Not, it must be admitted, the most exciting of Monaco Grands Prix but one which was certainly full of interest from start to finish and one which clearly indicated that, in their last year of life, the turbocars were still very much ahead of their 3½ litre rivals. Prost first, Berger second, Alboreto third and Warwick fourth with only the top three going the full 78 lap distance. And if the turbos were that far ahead at sea-level Monaco the 'atmospheric' teams weren't going to see which way they went at the 7,000 feet altitude of Mexico in two weeks' time!

MONACO GRAND PRIX

Winner: Alain Prost, McLaren-Honda MP4/4-04   *Fastest Lap:* Ayrton Senna, 86.260 mph

GRID POSITION

No.	Driver
12	Senna
11	Prost
28	Berger
27	Alboreto
5	Mansell
19	Nannini
17	Warwick
6	Patrese
18	Cheever
3	Palmer
1	Piquet
14	Streiff
30	Alliot
15	Gugelmin
24	Sala
20	Boutsen
36	Caffi
32	Larrauri
22	De Cesaris
25	Arnoux
29	Dalmas
16	Capelli
9	Ghinzani
31	Tarquini
21	Larini
26	Johansson

RESULTS

Pos.	Driver	Car
1	Prost	McLaren-Honda MP4/4-04
2	Berger	Ferrari F187/88C-104
3	Alboreto	Ferrari F187/88C-103
4	Warwick	Arrows-Megatron A10B/02
5	Palmer	Tyrrell-Cosworth DG/017-1
6	Patrese	Williams-Judd FW12/2
7	Dalmas	Lola-Cosworth LC88-02
8	Boutsen	Benetton-Ford B188-04
9	Larini	Osella-Alfa FA1L
10	Capelli	March-Judd 881/3

WORLD CHAMPIONSHIP

Drivers	Pts
1. Prost	24
2. Berger	14
3. Senna	9
4. Piquet	8
5. Alboreto	6
6. Warwick	6
7. Boutsen	3
8. Palmer	2
9. Nannini	1
Nakajima	1
Patrese	1

Constructors	Pts
1. McLaren-Honda	33
2. Ferrari	20
3. Lotus-Honda	9
4. Arrows-Megatron	6
5. Benetton-Ford	4
6. Tyrrell-Cosworth	2
7. Williams-Judd	1

29th May 1988
Circuit: Autodromo Hermanos Rodriguez

Mexico

NOWADAYS there are six 'long haul' Grands Prix which contribute to the World Championship's global image — Brazil, Mexico, Canada, America, Japan and Australia. They obviously involve an enormous amount of meticulous planning and detailed administration by the Formula One Constructors' Association (FOCA) and its individual team members for shifting nearly fifty race and spare cars with all their attendant engines, parts, equipment and personnel, thousands of miles around the world is no easy task. This year, unusually, four of the 'Outside Europe' races happened at the beginning of the season with Brazil, Mexico, Canada and America all in the first half dozen events. Hard work then for FOCA's Alan Woollard, the teams' transport managers and their specialist suppliers.

So after the glamour, colour, well-being and clean atmosphere of sea-level, money-soaked Monaco the teams travelled across the Atlantic Ocean to Central America and the squalor, heat, foul atmosphere and depression of Mexico City — most certainly not one of Grand Prix racing's most popular venues. Where, amidst the shattered city still slowly recovering from the hideous ravages of the 1986 earthquake, the high income life styles of Formula One contrast dramatically with those of the deprived sufferers of Mexico's sagging economy.

And to add to the misery of the normally-aspirated teams there's the major disadvantage of the altitude. For, at 7,000 feet, the smog-laden air is so thin that their engines, gasping for breath, have an added massive 27% power disadvantage against the turbocars whose engineers have only to make boost adjustments to maintain their horsepower.

So, at the flat 2.75 mile Autodromo Hermanos Rodriguez, with its long, very fast, straight and its sinuous series of bends, it was no surprise that the turbos dominated in practice — especially the McLarens. Senna, driving as though there was no tomorrow, took his fourth successive pole position of 1988 with a stupefying one minute 17.468 seconds lap — nearly a second faster than Nigel Mansell's 1987 four-bar time. With Prost second, Berger third (only one-tenth second slower), a much-happier-in-Mexico Nelson Piquet's

Top man 1987. Also ran 1988. All for want of Honda power.

Lotus-Honda fourth, Alboreto fifth and Satoru Nakajima his highest-ever at sixth ahead of Eddie Cheever's Arrows it was turbos at the front with a vengeance. But a magnificent eighth was the atmospheric Benetton of Alessandro Nannini — again

37

Off at 150 mph — but amazingly Alliot raced this Lola the next day.

faster that his team-mate Belgian Thierry Boutsen.

Last year's pole sitter and race winner Nigel Mansell was a despondent 14th on the grid and it was only his renowned bravery that got him there in a frightening-to-watch Williams whose Reactive suspension was totally at sea on the earthquake-rumpled surface of the Autodromo. But by far the most dramatic event of the four practice sessions was Philippe Alliot's terrifying crash on Saturday. Coming out of the notorious 150 mph Pits Turn Philippe completely lost his Lola-Ford which turned sharp right into the pit wall and then proceeded to barrel-roll down the straight — disintegrating as it did so. To everybody's amazed relief Alliot stepped out of the wreckage completely intact and to their even greater amazement the car was rebuilt in time to compete in Sunday's race!

There were actually five Mexican Grands Prix on Sunday — all of them engrossing in their different ways. The one for the two McLarens. The one for the Ferraris, with interference from the Lotuses of Piquet and Nakajima. The one for the Arrows. The one for the Benettons. And the one for the rest. The pity was that they never really looked like getting together.

After an aborted start caused by Nannini stalling his Benetton, Prost seized the race by the throat and shot into the lead the moment the lights changed. Senna, initially slowed by an errant pop-off valve, took second place from Piquet before the end of the first lap and from then on there was no change for the first two places with Prost masterfully maintaining a gap of some eight seconds between the McLarens.

But the man to watch was Berger. Revelling in the improved (but still inferior to the McLarens) performance of his Ferrari he shot past Piquet and into third place on lap nine and then grimly closed on Senna until half-distance when, heeding a 'low fuel'

Race 4 — MEXICO

reading, he backed off to lose touch. Totally unnecessarily as it sadly turned out for the gauge was faulty. Piquet then held his fourth place, easily coping with a threatening Michele Alboreto, until his Honda engine blew on lap 59. With Nelson's team-mate Satoru Nakajima long since retired from a fine sixth place with a broken turbo on lap 28 that was the end of Team Lotus's Mexican Grand Prix. And, thought many people, the renewal of their Honda contract for 1989.

So now it was Prost, Senna, Berger and Alboreto up front. McLaren, McLaren, Ferrari, Ferrari. And then the best fight of the race. Between those doughty Arrows rivals Derek Warwick and Eddie Cheever. For virtually the whole race there was nothing between them with first Cheever ahead and then, from lap 26, Warwick. And that was their finishing order. Fifth and sixth separated by seven-tenths of a second to give Arrows three valuable World Championship points.

Race four was the Benettons. Leading the 3½ litre category with Nannini ahead and driving magnificently to the vast discomfort, no doubt, of his longer-established team-mate Thierry Boutsen who, with balance and braking problems, trailed behind the Italian. The Benettons then were seventh and eighth. Fast, reliable and the best handling cars on the track. But, with no turbos, not fast enough.

And race five for the rest? In the end it was won by the very impressive Yannick Dalmas in his Lola — three laps down but a fine effort by the Frenchman who had patiently and capably worked his way up from his lowly 22nd place on the grid. And some encouragement for Gerard Larrousse's team after the expensive Alliot crashes at Monaco and Mexico. Encouragement too for Stefan Johansson who fought his Ligier into tenth place and for Bernd Schneider who, having at last started in a Grand Prix, had achieved an excellent eleventh place before he had to

For Riccardo, like Nigel, the Reactive suspension was disastrous. Thinking about it was worse! But then again perhaps he was thinking about something else — our photographer was!

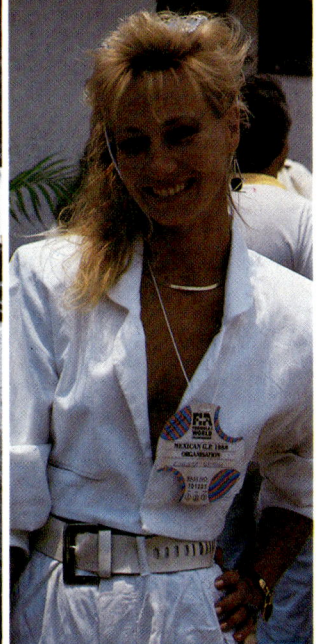

TEAM ANALYSIS

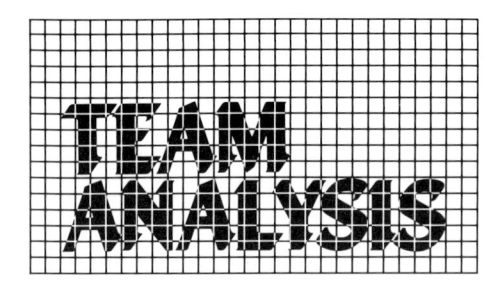

LOTUS
Race disappointment after practice satisfaction. After further suspension revisions to improve traction Piquet, at ease with 'fast' Mexico after unloved Monaco, qualifies encouraging fourth. Initially holds third place until passed by Berger, lap nine. Thereafter holds fourth, staving off Alboreto, until lap 59 when engine blows. Down to fifth — equal in Championship. Nakajima takes inspired highest-ever sixth on grid. Excellently improves to fourth, laps 1-2, before dropping to still-praiseworthy sixth laps 5-27. Retires with blown turbo lap 28. Team now third equal (with Arrows) in Constructors' Championship. But why do Honda engines win with McLaren but fail with Lotus?

TYRRELL
Definitely not worth the journey. For the first time since Austria 1985 both Tyrrells fail to qualify. Bailey goes off twice in ill-starred efforts to make grid. 'Just too slow' says Jonathan Palmer disheartened and depressed after magnificent Monaco drive.

WILLIAMS
Danger cones hoisted at Didcot after disastrous Mexico where Reactive suspension becomes hyper-active to make cars unhandleable. Very unhappy Nigel Mansell (pole position and first place in 1987) has suspension dangerously collapse on Friday — as does Patrese on Saturday. Showing great bravery Mansell qualifies 14th. Patrese equally gutsy 17th. Both retire from race with power loss. Mansell lap 21 after sliding back from initial eleventh to 19th. Patrese lap 17 from 15th. With car designed around Reactive system Williams face major corrective problem.

ZAKSPEED
Better in Mexico (it needed to be). With turbo advantage Ghinzani qualifies 18th — albeit behind eight NA cars. Advances to 13th (lapped) lap 28 before stopping to replace broken nosecone caused by spin. Finishes 15th (six laps down). Schneider qualifies well for first GP in 15th place in spite of being rammed by inevitable De Cesaris. Retires, lap 17, with overheated engine when strong eleventh.

McLAREN
Following catastrophic 1987 (both cars out by lap two) another victorious demonstration for 1988's fourth successive win and second 1/2. Prost qualifies second and leads the race from start to finish with record lap (one minute 18.61 secs) — faster than Piquet's 1987 four-bar time. Increases Championship lead over Berger to 15 points. Senna takes fourth successive pole (career 20th) faster than Mansell's 1987 time. Loses race before first corner when erratic pop-off valve causes temporary power loss. Finishes second with blistered rear tyres and low fuel to move within three points of second-place Berger in Championship. Both Prost and Senna lap everyone except Berger. After only four races team now lead Constructors' Championship by massive 21 points.

AGS
Streiff qualifies 19th. Climbs to eleventh by lap 28 but stops, lap 45, for new electronic control unit. Finishes 12th (four laps down). Team thus continues enormous improvement on 1987.

This year's AGS is most impressive. So is Philippe Streiff.

MARCH
Fortified by $4m cash injection from Japanese Leyton House sponsor team continues steady improvement. After qualifying 16th with Friday time Gugelmin advances to 14th before retiring with overheated backside due to battery fire! Impressive Capelli second fastest NA car on grid (10th) but after bad start loses three laps in pits freeing jammed gear selectors. Finishes 16th (six laps down).

ARROWS
Mexico continues Arrows team's impressivve 1988 renaissance. Cheever and Warwick qualify seventh and ninth and then enjoy superb race-long wheel to wheel battle which ends with them finishing excellent fifth (Warwick) and sixth (one lap down) only three-tenths of second apart in Team's first 1988 'both in points' race. With three points finishes Warwick retains fifth equal Championship place. Arrows advance to third equal (with Lotus) in Constructors' Championship.

BENETTON
At circuit where team at enormous disadvantage due to altitude, Benetton consolidate their position as top NA contestants. Nannini again out-qualifies Boutsen in superb eighth place as top NA ahead of four turbocars. Boutsen eleventh on grid. Nannini causes first start to be aborted by

Race 4 — MEXICO

Without a wing (or a prayer!). Arnoux limps back.

stalling on line. Benetton teamsters then run reliably throughout race to finish top NA cars. Nannini seventh (two laps down) in spite of broken helmet strap and recurrence of Monaco foot-pain problem. Trailing Boutsen eighth (minus three laps) with handling deficiencies.

OSELLA
Larini fails to qualify due to electrical malfunction.

RIAL
De Cesaris maintains shameful record by ramming Schneider in practice. Then qualifies well at 12th. Moves up one place in race before retiring, lap 10, after failed clutch leads to gearbox break up.

MINARDI
Campos non-qualifies with broken gearbox input shaft. At first Mexican GP Sala, now unquestionably Minardi number one, just makes grid at 25th. Stalls on line but after push start drives steady race to finish 11th (four laps down). After their unsuccessful years with Motor Moderni engines, however, for Minardi to finish is good.

LIGIER
After tests show that modified 1987 JS29 slower than unsuccessful 1988 JS31 Ligier decide to persevere with problematic '88 car. To little avail. Arnoux qualifies 20th and Johansson 24th. In race Arnoux rammed by Caffi to retire when 20th, lap 14, minus rear wing. Johansson 'finds a rhythm for the first time this year' and finishes tenth (four laps down).

FERRARI
Engine modifications intended for Monaco appear at Mexico. Revised 'Honda-type' induction system and cylinder heads reduce power gap to Honda to estimated 35 hp. Maranello reportedly riven by dissension and politics but cars obviously better. Berger qualifies excellent third only one-tenth slower than Prost. Drives another fine race challenging Senna for second until obliged to back-off due to 'low fuel' reading which later turns out to be incorrect. Finishes third — in points for fourth successive race — and only runner to go full distance with two McLarens. Retains second place in Drivers' Championship. Alboreto fifth on grid and races to finish fourth, one lap down. Improves to fourth in Championship. Team still second in Constructors' Championship but now depressing 21 points behind McLaren.

LOLA
Lola's Mexico dominated by massive Alliot practice shunt at notorious 150 mph Pits Turn which amazingly fails either to destroy car or injure driver. Alliot qualifies 13th and after stalling on grid starts from the back in even more amazingly rebuilt crashed car (no spare after Alliot Monaco crash). Then retires at end of lap one with cracked rear suspension upright. Dalmas 22nd on grid but races steadily and well to finish ninth (three laps down).

COLONI
After failing to pre-qualify Tarquini allowed to practice when Modena excluded. Qualifies 21st. Keeps running to finish 14th (three laps down).

EUROBRUN
Modena excluded in Friday pre-qualifying for too-wide rear wing. Larrauri just scrapes in at 26th but finishes GP for first time in 13th place (four laps down).

DALLARA
Caffi starts 23rd. Retires lap 14 after ramming Arnoux Ligier when brakes fail.

Montezuma's Revenge!? No, just a new Mexican custom for the hard-working teams.

FOUR TOP TEAMS FINISH IN PERFECT SYMMETRY...

McLaren first and second...

Ferrari third and fourth...

retire on lap 17. Mexico may have provided some reward for all of them but for 1987 winner Nigel Mansell and Riccardo Patrese in their Williams-Judds it was a mixture of misery, bruising and fright. After unsuccessfully trying to tame their foul-handling cars during the two days of practice they both took early planes after retiring with an acute loss of power. After four Grands Prix Williams, the dominant Constructors' Champions of 1987, had only scored one point.

It would be wrong to say that the 1988 Mexico Grand Prix was exciting. To the casual observer it was a case of Prost and Senna first and second all the way and with no change in the top five from laps ten to fifty-nine. But to the afficionados it was a very significant race. Partly because 16 of the

Race 4 — MEXICO

26 starters were classified as finishers (61.5% is good? Well it is by Grand Prix standards!) but more so because of the way Alain Prost achieved his 31st World Championship victory. After Monaco a lot of people who should know better were suggesting that he was already 'yesterday's man' and that from now on it would be Senna in charge. But Prost led from the start in Mexico, controlled the race from the front, showed that he most certainly hadn't lost any of his magical touch and created a new lap record in the process — at 125.8 mph nearly a full second faster than Nelson Piquet's previous record with four-bar boost and some 200 more horsepower.

Before the Mexican Grand Prix in his hungry quest for his first World Championship Ayrton Senna needed to win the next five races (with Prost finishing second) even to draw level with Alain. Now, eighteen points behind, he needed to win the next six . . .

Arrows fifth and sixth . . .

Benetton seventh and eighth.

43

MURRAY WALKER'S GRAND PRIX YEAR

Mexico '88 — victory number 31 for Alain Prost.

MEXICO GRAND PRIX

Winner: Alain Prost, McLaren-Honda MP4/4-04 **Fastest Lap:** Alain Prost, 125.808 mph

GRID POSITION

No.	Driver
12	Senna
11	Prost
28	Berger
1	Piquet
27	Alboreto
2	Nakajima
18	Cheever
19	Nannini
17	Warwick
16	Capelli
20	Boutsen
22	De Cesaris
30	Alliot
5	Mansell
10	Schneider
15	Gugelmin
6	Patrese
9	Ghinzani
14	Streiff
25	Arnoux
31	Tarquini
29	Dalmas
36	Caffi
26	Johansson
24	Sala
32	Larrauri

RESULTS

Pos.	Driver	Car
1	Prost	McLaren-Honda MP4/4-04
2	Senna	McLaren-Honda MP4/4-01
3	Berger	Ferrari F187/88C-104
4	Alboreto	Ferrari F187/88C-103
5	Warwick	Arrows-Megatron A10B/02
6	Cheever	Arrows-Megatron A10B/01
7	Nannini	Benetton-Ford B188-03
8	Boutsen	Benetton-Ford B188-04
9	Dalmas	Lola-Cosworth LC88-02
10	Johansson	Ligier-Judd JS31/03
11	Sala	Minardi-Cosworth M188-03
12	Streiff	AGS-Cosworth JH23/2
13	Larrauri	EuroBrun-Cosworth 188-02
14	Tarquini	Coloni-Cosworth 188-FC02
15	Ghinzani	Zakspeed 883/4
16	Capelli	March-Judd 881/3

WORLD CHAMPIONSHIP

Drivers	Pts
1. Prost	33
2. Berger	18
3. Senna	15
4. Alboreto	9
5. Piquet	8
Warwick	8
7. Boutsen	3
8. Palmer	2
9. Nannini	1
Nakajima	1
Patrese	1
Cheever	1

Constructors	Pts
1. McLaren-Honda	48
2. Ferrari	27
3. Lotus-Honda	9
Arrows-Megatron	9
5. Benetton-Ford	4
6. Tyrrell-Cosworth	2
7. Williams-Judd	1

44

12th June 1988
Circuit: Gilles Villeneuve, Montreal

Canada

THANKFULLY from Mexico to Montreal they went. For the cars a twenty-one truck, seven day journey from the place the teams like least to one of the places they like most. And no wonder. Montreal is a beautiful place with none of Mexico City's depressing attributes and, as ever, there was an enthusiastic welcome for the teams who were cautiously expecting closer competition than there had been at the Autodromo Hermanos Rodriquez. For the 2.74 mile circuit on a man-made island in the St Lawrence Seaway is not only at sea level, which eliminates the extra 'altitude' penalty the atmospheric cars suffer at Mexico, but is also, with its 31 gear changes a lap and frequent braking and acceleration, notoriously hard on fuel consumption. Harder even than Imola. So in Canada it was hoped that the 3½ litre teams, notably Benetton, Williams, March and Lola, would be more competitive than they had thus far. But that's what they'd hoped at Monaco!

When the teams arrived in Montreal they found a much-modified Gilles Villeneuve Circuit. In 1987 there had been no race there because of a squabble about who held the organisation and sponsorship rights but now, to everyone's great delight, it was not only back but better. From its inception the circuit had had no proper garages and the teams had had to do their demanding work in the open. In the two year interval since the last Canadian GP, however, the organisers had spent a lot and done a lot to

Good to be back — start of the first Canadian Grand Prix since 1986.

45

improve it and its facilities by providing fine new permanent garages, an imposing control tower and a widened start and finish straight.

To mark the occasion — and with no disrespect to McLaren who's dedicated work and fine chassis, allied to the brilliance of Prost and Senna and Honda-power, had won them every 1988 Grand Prix so far — most people were hoping for a change of personnel on the podium at the end of the race. 'But,' said Alain Prost 'our job is to win. You can hardly expect us to slow down to stop people getting bored!'

In Canada though maybe it wasn't going to be so easy. For during the two days of practice it rapidly became clear that fuel consumption was going to be even more critical than people had thought. But that would be during the race As usual the two McLarens were in a class of their own during the two qualifying sessions and when the flag went out at two o'clock on Saturday afternoon it was Senna in pole position for the fifth time in five races (four seconds inside Nigel Mansell's 1986 time) with Prost alongside him. Berger and Alboreto were again third and fourth in their Ferraris but then it was Nannini and Boutsen in their 3½ litre Benettons sandwiching Nelson Piquet's turbocharged Lotus-Honda. In fact the Benettons, with 215 litre tanks were looking good which is more than could be said for the perplexed Williams team whose two thoroughly disgruntled drivers were in only ninth and eleventh places. For both Mansell (ninth) and Patrese had found the Reactive suspension to be little better in Canada than it had been in Mexico and were certainly not relishing the thought of 69 laps around the bumpy Island track.

Derek Warwick was relishing the thought even less. On Saturday he had had the most enormous 'off' in his Arrows which had left him badly bruised and shaken with fears of torn back ligaments. Typically, after a medical check had pronounced him fit enough to drive he decided to do so notwithstanding massive discomfort.

On Sunday it really did look as though an 'Atmospheric' win was possible. The weather was hot — 29 degrees — and windy. Worried Honda technicians had told their McLaren and Lotus drivers not to exceed 2.3 bar boost and 11,000 rpm (out of a possible 13,000) and Lotus had further decided to run with the minimum wing in order to reduce drag. But funnily enough the man you'd have thought would be best pleased — Benetton Manager Peter Collins — was tipping McLaren for victory. How right he was!

Off into the wide blue yonder motored Alain Prost taking full advantage of the fact that although he was second on the grid he had actually got the best starting position — a fact which the unhappy Ayrton Senna had forcefully pointed out to anyone who would listen, but about which the Race Officials regarded themselves as powerless to do anything.

So it was the now very familiar sight of the red and white Woking cars in the lead with the Ferraris of Berger and Alboreto trying to keep up. Berger did so for just ten laps before his fuel read out told him that if he didn't slow down he wouldn't finish. So he slowed down. And past him swept both Boutsen and Nannini who had already disposed of Alboreto. Then on lap nineteen we saw something we hadn't seen all season — a McLaren passing a McLaren! For several laps Senna had been looking for an opportunity to have a go at Prost and when they came up to lap backmarkers he got it. 'Ayrton is much braver than me in traffic,' said Alain afterwards, 'he will dive in without hesitation where I would rather wait and he did so here. It was a fair move and I've no complaint. I suppose I could have blocked him but that's not my way.' And there speaks not only a Gentleman but the World's top driver. It's a pity some of his colleagues don't think and act the same way.

So the two McLarens led the two Benettons with the two Ferraris next up followed by Piquet with Mansell on his gearbox and looking for a way past his unbeloved late team-mate. Which he found on lap 23. But before that the hard charging Nannini had departed the scene when he sadly rolled to a standstill with drowned electrics caused by, of all things, a split hose.

And then the Ferraris disappeared. Berger's engine 'just stopped' on lap 23 and it subsequently turned out that an incorrect

Race 5 — CANADA

DESIGNER CARS 1988?

Rory Byrne's
Benetton-Ford

Gerard Ducarouge's
Lotus-Honda

Eric Zakowski's
Zakspeed

Adrian Newey's
March-Judd

TEAM ANALYSIS

LOTUS
A lacklustre meeting amidst worrying rumours about the future of the 30 year old team. Piquet, first in Canada in 1982 and '84, qualifies only sixth. Races with reduced grip due to need to conserve fuel by running with minimum wing and, therefore, downforce. Offers no challenge to McLarens and Ferraris, and is passed by both NA Benettons and Mansell's Williams. Finishes unimpressive fourth (lapped) following retirements ahead but improves to fourth in Championship. Nakajima, in first race in Canada, qualifies lowly 13th and takes eleventh place, three laps down.

TYRRELL
Good for Palmer. Bad for Bailey. With new, stiffer monocoque Palmer qualifies 19th and then drives another excellent and gritty race to finish in the points at sixth (two laps down) despite having to play footsie with loose drink container. At eighth, now second NA driver in Championship. Seemingly jinxed Bailey starts second GP 23rd in 'flexible' Tyrrell only to smite Sala's Minardi at start and withdraw immediately with broken suspension.

Palmer sixth in spite of mobile cockpit drinks cannister!

WILLIAMS
Another awful race. Reactive suspension, reviled by both drivers, suits Canada little better than Mexico. Both Mansell and Patrese qualify with Friday times. Nigel ninth and Riccardo eleventh. Mansell determinedly improves to fifth (including passing Piquet's turbo Lotus) on lap 23 but retires, lap 29, with solid Judd engine. Still no points. Patrese harmlessly collides with Cheever at first corner and retires from ninth place, lap 33, also with duff Judd.

ZAKSPEED
Still struggling. Ghinzani starts 22nd and races at rear of field with overheating engine to take last classified position, 14th, six laps down. Unfortunate Schneider again fails to qualify (fourth time in five races) due to engine problems.

McLAREN
Alone amongst the eighteen competing Constructors McLaren again gets it totally right with their fifth win, fifth pole, fourth grid 1/2, third race 1/2 and fourth fastest lap of 1988. Senna takes fifth successive pole, wins race after catching and passing faster-starting Prost, and breaks lap record (one minute 24.973 = 115.57 mph) to move to second in Championship albeit 15 points behind Prost. After yielding lead Prost, more cautious than Senna when passing slower drivers and concerned about fuel consumption and overheating engine, settles for six points and gloomily contemplates next week's Detroit race which he hates and which Senna won in both 1986 and 1987. McLaren lead of Constructors' Championship now a stupefying 36 points.

AGS
Automobiles Gonfaronaise Sportive, one of Grand Prix's smallest teams with but fifteen employees, continues to humble larger and more experienced rivals. Lanky Philippe Streiff qualifies excellent tenth (fourth fastest NA) and, benefiting from retirements, races up to a very impressive fifth — determinedly challenging Piquet for fourth for eight laps. Retires, lap 42, after spinning and damaging rear suspension.

MARCH
Like several teams, first time at Montreal. Capelli starts 14th and drives excellent race to finish fifth after lengthy battles with Patrese, De Cesaris, Modena and Alliot and score first personal and team Championship points for 1988. Gugelmin qualifies 18th with handling problems. Races towards rear of field hampered by cockpit interference from loose Longines box which causes missed gears. Resultant gearbox damage forces retirement lap 55.

ARROWS
Derek Warwick involved in gigantic Saturday practice crash at new bends entering start/finish straight. After medical check bravely starts from 16th on grid and, in great discomfort, steadily races up through field to inspired seventh place. Eddie Cheever qualifies strong eighth (although behind both NA Benettons). Collides with Patrese on first lap and then slides back with overheating engine. Retires from 13th place (lap 32: broken throttle linkage) after long battle with team-mate Warwick.

BENETTON
Team, which had never scored points in Canada, strongly fancied to do well — partly because of its 215 litre fuel tanks. Turns out to be the class of the field apart from all-conquering McLarens. Nannini qualifies magnificent fifth and Boutsen excellent seventh (in new chassis). Boutsen, followed by Nannini, passes both Ferraris to very impressive third place — top NA car — which he retains to

Race 5 — CANADA

race end as only driver other than Senna and Prost to go full distance. Similarly fine Nannini drive terminated when retires from fifth, lap 16, due to split hose drowning ignition.

OSELLA
For fourth time in five races Larini fails to qualify due this time to Friday shunt and subsequent lack of grip.

RIAL
So very nearly two points for the new German team in its fifth race! After his usual dodgem-cars practice (this time into Alliot's Lola) De Cesaris qualifies well at twelfth and races even better to a very impressive fifth place on lap 42, having disposed of Capelli, Patrese and Cheever and battled against Streiff and Piquet. But with only a 185 litre tank runs out of fuel with just three laps to go. Classified ninth.

MINARDI
Campos fails to qualify for his first Canadian GP amidst rumours that he is for the chop. Sala, also first time in Canada, starts 21st. Rear wing removed in start line confrontation with Bailey. Rejoins after repairs and races reliably at rear of field to finish 13th five laps down.

LIGIER
With no time between Mexico and Canada for desperately needed improvements cars still gripless. Arnoux and Johansson qualify 20th and 25th. After collisions with Tarquini and Larrauri Arnoux retires with broken gearbox, lap 37. Johansson, grappling as usual with massive understeer, lasts until lap 25 when retires from 17th place with failed Judd engine.

FERRARI
Team at very low ebb due to Maranello politics. With revised plenum chambers and pistons Berger and Alboreto qualify third and fourth. Resigned Berger holds third to McLarens until lap 14 when passed by both Benettons. Retires, lap 23, when engine stops due, it transpires, to fitment of incorrect ECU chip! Alboreto, similarly taken by Boutsen and Nannini, lasts in fourth place after Berger and Nannini retirements until lap 34 when engine fails. A sad decline after Team's 1987 revival.

Locked up — Alliot's Lola makes quick arrest.

LOLA
Dalmas, at first Canadian GP, hits wall and wrecks car on Friday. Fails to qualify in car rebuilt from Alliot Mexico crash. Alliot, fully recovered after Mexico, starts 17th and progresses vigorously through field to seventh place before running out of fuel on lap 67. Classified tenth.

COLONI
Tarquini qualifies last at 26th for first Canadian GP. With reliable drive and despite a spin and later collision with Arnoux gives team highest-ever finish at heartening eighth (two laps down).

EUROBRUN
At last Modena proves his class. Qualifies excellent 15th first time in Canada. In pretty ho-hum car forces up to superb seventh on lap 42 before having to stop for adjustment of gear selectors. Rejoins to finish twelfth, three laps down. Larrauri leap-frogs on and off track to qualify car-shattered 24th. Rams Arnoux (biter bit!) and retires less nosecone on lap nine.

DALLARA
With gearbox problems Caffi fails to pre-qualify on Friday morning.

Despite practice shunt, Modena qualified a superb 15th.

49

MURRAY WALKER'S GRAND PRIX YEAR

electronic control unit chip and been fitted! Somebody's head will have rolled no doubt — to join those which had already done so at Maranello where all was misery and strife. And on lap 34 a now thoroughly dispirited Michele, totally disenchanted with his lot at Ferrari, wearily emerged from his stationary car which had broken its engine.

Behind the processional Senna, Prost and Boutsen though things were well worth watching. For as Senna put in a searing lap in one minute 24.97 seconds (115.57 mph) to break Piquet's 1986 four-bar record by half a second Nelson, short of grip as a result of the decision to run with minimum wing, was fighting to hold fourth place in front of the very effective AGS of a quite magnificent Philippe Streiff. And right behind Philippe were De Cesaris (RIAL), Capelli (March) and Modena (EuroBrun). De Cesaris? And Modena? Yes indeed and both of them driving superbly. Especially Modena who had had the cruel luck to be excluded from two previous races through no fault of his

So nearly in the points — De Cesaris had a fine race after a stone punctured his Rial in practice.

Messrs Stanbury, Mainwaring and Hallam (in yellow) from Team Lotus contemplate aerodynamics of (March coloured!) vessel for Mechanics Raft Race. Over-aspirated Team Tyrrell won the event!

Race 5 — CANADA

TV camera missing nothing — this time Alboreto's Ferrari.

and was now showing his undoubted class by forcing his dumpy car to go much faster than anyone had thought possible. Including, I suspect, its designer!

But what of the two Williams men? Both out. Just six laps after he'd had the grim satisfaction of passing Piquet, Mansell felt his Judd engine saying goodbye and rolled to standstill at the entrance to the pit lane to retire from his fifth successive race. And five laps later Patrese withdrew at his pit for the same reason. Which, despite John Judd's untiring efforts to get things right, no doubt confirmed the team's view that they'd been wise to sign with Renault to use their new V10 engine for the next three years.

Meanwhile up at the front Senna and Prost continued on their victorious way, now with any pressure that they might have been under, long since removed. For Boutsen knew full well that there was no way that he could catch either of them and had happily settled for third place — which he not only took, but did so by going the whole distance. Which is more than anyone else did. Fourth was a lapped Piquet but poor Philippe Streiff overdid it in his inspired efforts to get past the Lotus and spun out of contention leaving Ivan Capelli to take a well deserved fifth place ahead of a very surprised Jonathan Palmer — thanks to De Cesaris running out of fuel with just two laps to go.

Another 'interesting' race for the enthusiast but sadly not one that would have fired the imagination and enthusiasm of the world's uncommitted TV viewers. Except, perhaps, the magnificent drive of the battered Derek Warwick who finished the race drained and exhausted in a quite superb seventh place. Never mind, maybe it would be different at Detroit's street circuit next week. That really was somewhere where the Atmospheric cars could show the McLarens the way home wasn't it? Well wasn't it?

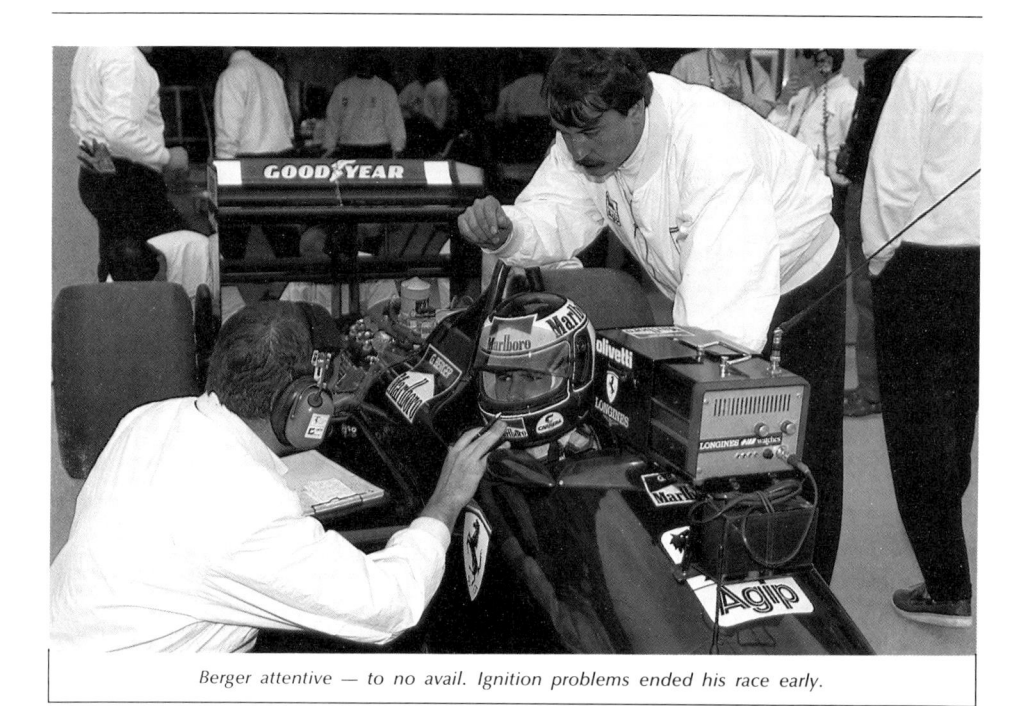

Berger attentive — to no avail. Ignition problems ended his race early.

CANADIAN GRAND PRIX

Winner: Ayrton Senna, McLaren-Honda MP4/4-01 **Fastest Lap:** Ayrton Senna, 115.567 mph

GRID POSITION			RESULTS			WORLD CHAMPIONSHIP			
No.	Driver	Pos. Driver	Car	Drivers	Pts	Constructors	Pts
12	Senna	1 Senna	McLaren-Honda MP4/4-01	1. Prost	39	1. McLaren-Honda	63
11	Prost	2 Prost	McLaren-Honda MP4/4-04	2. Senna	24	2. Ferrari	27
28	Berger	3 Boutsen	Benetton-Ford B188-05	3. Berger	18	3. Lotus-Honda	12
27	Alboreto	4 Piquet	Lotus-Honda 100T/2	4. Piquet	11	4. Arrows-Megatron	9
19	Nannini	5 Capelli	March-Judd 881/3	5. Alboreto	9	5. Benetton-Ford	8
1	Piquet	6 Palmer	Tyrrell-Cosworth DG/017-4	6. Warwick	8	6. Tyrrell-Cosworth	3
20	Boutsen	7 Warwick	Arrows-Megatron A10B/02	7. Boutsen	7	7. March-Judd	2
18	Cheever	8 Tarquini	Coloni-Cosworth 188-FC02	8. Palmer	3	8. Williams-Judd	1
5	Mansell	9 De Cesaris	Rial-Cosworth ARC1/01	9. Capelli	2		
14	Streiff	10 Alliot	Lola-Cosworth LC88-04	10. Cheever	1		
6	Patrese	11 Nakajima	Lotus-Honda 100T/4	Nakajima	1		
22	De Cesaris	12 Modena	EuroBrun-Cosworth 188-03	Nannini	1		
2	Nakajima	13 Sala	Minardi-Cosworth M188-03	Patrese	1		
16	Capelli	14 Ghinzani	Zakspeed 881/4				
33	Modena						
17	Warwick						
30	Alliot						
15	Gugelmin						
3	Palmer						
25	Arnoux						
24	Sala						
9	Ghinzani						
4	Bailey						
32	Larrauri						
26	Johansson						
31	Tarquini						

19th June 1988
Circuit: Detroit

USA East

MOST people regard Grand Prix life as being exciting and glamorous and there's no denying that it is. But even under normal circumstances it exerts heavy pressures on its participants and is very demanding and tiring — especially for the drivers and mechanics. The circumstances at Detroit, however, were distinctly abnormal.

By the time the teams arrived in America by way of Mexico and Canada for round six of the championship and having already been out of Europe to Brazil at the beginning of the season, they had been away from their bases for three weeks, living out of suitcases and divorced from their HQ rebuilding and preparation facilities. You might think therefore that 'high-tech' America would be a very welcome temporary home but, for very different reasons, they were little happier in Motown than they had been in Mexico.

You see Detroit, like Monaco, is a street circuit and like Monaco it has no pitlane garages which means that the on-track working conditions for the mechanics are onerous — as they are for the drivers too. The city streets which make up the 2.5 mile circuit are used by very heavy everyday traffic for the rest of the year and they are further badly affected by Michigan's bitter winter weather. The result is that they are bumpy, slippery and dangerous but, to make things worse, they break up when subjected to the tearing stresses of Formula One tyres and horsepower. With twenty corners — many of them right angles — and 58 gear changes to the lap, allied to incessant breaking and accelerating as they try to stick to the fastest line without hitting the ever-present unyielding concrete walls or getting on to the 'marbles' the drivers regard Detroit as a joke in poor taste. They are also irritated by the fact that, because of the nature of the circuit, America is presented with an inferior Grand Prix spectacle and dispirited by the fact that downtown Detroit City is definitely short on atmosphere and charisma. So no one was unhappy to learn that this was to be the last time its Grand Prix would be held on the existing six year old circuit. Next year it moves to a purpose-built new 2.8 mile track constructed on Belle Isle a few miles from

In the shades of Goodyear's tireless team heads — Barry Griffin and Lee Gaug — Nigel Mansell reflects.

the city. But this was this year, and things seemed no better than they had been before.

The oppressive temperatures that were affecting much of America were certainly affecting Detroit. It was hot. Very hot. The combination of the heat and the basically inadequate road surface meant that the already difficult conditions were made worse. If you weren't out with the intention of putting up a fast time in the first ten minutes of Saturday's qualifying hour you might just as well stay in the pit lane and hope that your Friday time wouldn't be beaten, for the slithery tarmac and broken

53

Minardi and Martini no hopers? Not in Detroit — the first GP point for both of them.

surface prevented any improvement later in the session.

A worrying by-product of the conditions was that there were inevitably several rapid off-course excursions — two of which could well have had worse results than fortunately they did. Ivan Capelli slammed his March into and along the pit wall as he exited the left/right riverfront chicane after the tunnel, and several officials, mechanics and onlookers were hit by flying debris. Fortunately no one was seriously hurt but Capelli's resultant cracked foot bone prevented his racing the next day. Stefano Modena also had to be taken to hospital for a check after he had lost traction and smashed backwards into the concrete barrier at Turn Six. He raced the next day wearing a neck support brace.

When the grid formed on Sunday there was an unfamiliar look about it. Only one McLaren in the front row for the first time since Brazil! Unsurprisingly it was Senna's who, relaxed and confident at the circuit where he had won for the past two years, made one of his 'total commitment' laps on Friday to circulate in one minute 40.6 seconds — 1.4 seconds slower than Nigel Mansell's 1987 pole time. Puzzled by what he had felt was a much faster time, he then discovered that his turbo boost adjuster had been in the 'low' position! Saturday's conditions prevented his going any faster in the final qualifying session but still no one beat him. Behind Ayrton it was the welcome sight of two Ferraris — Berger's and Alboreto's — going better in Detroit than they had in Canada but with two very unhappy drivers concerned about their ability to cope with the crumbling track — concern which turned out to be all too well founded. Prost, making no attempt to hide his dislike for Detroit, was fourth followed by the top 'atmospherics' — Boutsen's Benetton, Mansell's Williams (still with major Reactive suspension problems) and Nannini's Benetton ahead of World Champion Nelson Piquet's turbo-charged Lotus-Honda. There was nobody on the grid who hadn't had car or circuit problems during practice and there was nobody who was eagerly anticipating the nearly two hours of exhausting driving and unremitting concentration that the 63 laps would require.

Like Canada, the weekend before, the story of the first place is easily and quickly

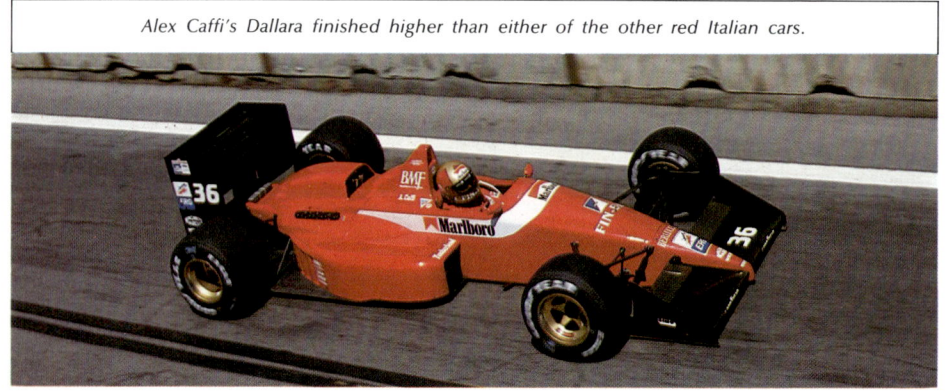

Alex Caffi's Dallara finished higher than either of the other red Italian cars.

Race 6 — USA EAST

Pretty cars all in a row.

55

TEAM ANALYSIS

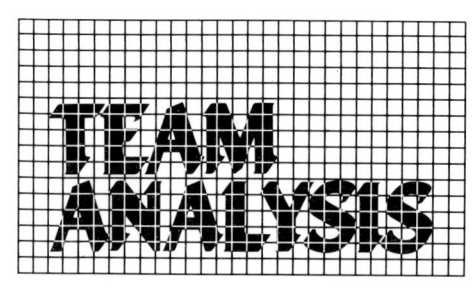

Nelson dislikes street circuits — his race ended on lap 27.

LOTUS
Canada was bad but Detroit was worse. After crashing spare car on Friday Piquet (1984 winner) qualifies only eighth behind three NA cars. In ninth place at circuit he dislikes Nelson stops for tyres on lap 24 and then spins into wall, lap 27. No points and now shares Championship fourth place with Boutsen. Nakajima totally fails to cope with Detroit and does not qualify. Team Lotus poor third equal with Benetton in Constructors' Championship.

TYRRELL
Another inspired drive by Jonathan Palmer who, after qualifying 17th with understeer, has to stop at end of lap one to replace front wing bent against Larrauri's EuroBrun. Thereafter magnificently fights through field to finish fighting fifth one lap down with sticking throttle (third points finish of 1988 — a triumph of driver over car). At eighth place second NA driver in Championship. Bailey starts 22nd for third GP. Drives sensible and steady race to take first finish (ninth: four laps down) although fails to cross line through sliding into wall on last lap due to sheer exhaustion.

WILLIAMS
Another disaster after reasonably encouraging practice in which Mansell qualifies sixth and Patrese tenth after continued unhappiness with inadequately developed Reactive suspension for FW12 chassis. Mansell car transmission fails on parade lap forcing him to start in spare. Grittily advances to fourth but retires for sixth time in six races when engine cuts out on lap 19. Patrese takes over fourth place until his engine also cuts out to force lap 27 retirement. Hopefully two week gap before French GP will enable essential remedy to be found.

ZAKSPEED
1988 season misery intensified when both Ghinzani and Schneider fail to qualify.

McLAREN
In past Detroit had not been McLaren lucky circuit but 1988 sees continuance of season's overwhelming success record. Senna takes sixth successive pole to equal Stirling Moss and Niki Lauda record and then leads race from start to finish to win third consecutive Detroit GP. Second in Championship behind Prost with reduced gap of twelve points. Prost qualifies fourth at circuit he detests. After poor start races past Boutsen, Alboreto and Berger up to second on lap six where he finishes hampered by slow tyre stop and gearchange difficulties but makes fastest lap (one minute 44.84 seconds = 85.85 mph). Both drivers lap all other competitors. McLaren Constructors' Championship lead now demoralising 51 points.

AGS
Streiff qualifies his AGS, now one of top 3½ litre cars, eleventh. Impressively advances to seventh, lap 15, but hits Piquet Lotus on the way and retires, lap 16, with broken rear suspension.

MARCH
Capelli has alarming accident on Saturday morning when he hits and slides along pit wall. Non starts with broken foot bone. Gugelmin has best GP yet progressing from 13th at start to fine fifth on lap 27 (convincingly passing Piquet on way). Retains place until lap 35 when retires with blown Judd engine.

ARROWS
Worst race yet in encouraging year. Warwick starts well at ninth in spite of breathing difficulties after Canada crash and being assaulted by Grand Prix's 'bovver boy' Andrea De Cesaris. Up to seventh by lap seven but retires lap 27 after hitting wall when throttle sticks open. Cheever qualifies 15th but retires lap 15 (overheating) after improving to eleventh. Team drops place to fifth in Constructors' Championship.

Ayrton Senna masterfully won his third consecutive Detroit Grand Prix.

Race 6 — USA EAST

BENETTON
Ford-powered team thankfully do well at Ford Worldwide HQ. Boutsen qualifies fifth and top NA car. Third by lap eight and, delighted with car, stays there for second race in succession (lapped by Senna/Prost). Jumps three places to fourth equal (with Piquet) and top NA driver in Championship. Nannini starts seventh. With failing brakes inadvertently nudges Alboreto into spin. Thereby improves to fourth but retires, lap 15, with damaged suspension following Ferrari contact. Benetton now distant third equal (top NA) with Lotus in Constructors' Championship.

OSELLA
Larini fails to qualify but starts as a result of Capelli withdrawal. Retires from 23rd, lap eight, with blown engine.

RIAL
An excellent race to give RIAL their first Championship points in only their sixth race. After usual practice barging match (into Warwick and hit by Dalmas) De Cesaris starts twelfth. With most impressive drive achieves sixth place by lap 15 and finishes well-merited fourth (one lap down). some recompense for the lost fifth place in Montreal.

MINARDI
Minardi's first ever World Championship point in 52 races and from a 'new' driver! Pierluigi Martini, discarded in 1986, returns to team in place of rejected Adrian Campos. Benefiting from two successful seasons of Formula 3000 Martini qualifies well at 16th and then drives excellent race to finish sixth in his first GP since Australia 1985. Sala scrapes in at 26th but races steadily and well until lap 55 retirement (clutch).

LIGIER
Revised suspension but still no grip. Johansson and Arnoux qualify 18th and 20th. Johansson dispiritedly retires lap three with exhausted qualifying engine. Arnoux, struggling with overheated Judd motor, improves to seventh following multiple retirements but has to retire, lap 46, when Judd expires.

FERRARI
Encouraging practice. Discouraging race. Amidst continuing political uproar (ailing 90-year-old Enzo Ferrari shortly to announce revised Team Management structure after sacking his son Piero Lardi Ferrari) Berger and Alboreto qualify well at second and third. Berger second laps 1-5 until passed by Prost. Retires from third, lap seven, with puncture caused by contact with Boutsen's Benetton. Alboreto nudged into spin by nearly brakeless Nannini when fourth on lap eight. Recovers and fights up to seventh but retires, lap 46, when engine blows.

LOLA
With only two chassis for Team after Canada Alliot starts 14th and Dalmas 25th. Hampered by brake problems Alliot retires from ninth lap 47 with broken transmission. Dalmas again impresses with seventh place (two laps down) out of eight finishers.

The track with the 'marbles' surface — once again the streets of Detroit broke up under F1 pressures.

COLONI
For first time in Team's debut full season Tarquini fails to pre-qualify.

EUROBRUN
As in Canada both drivers qualify — Modena 19th and Larrauri 24th (Modena in spite of Saturday practice crash which necessitates hospital check). Both cars adversely affected by gear selector problems in race causing Larrauri retirement on lap 27 and Modena to stop twice for attention. Modena subsequently retires, lap 47, after hitting wall.

DALLARA
Excellent and encouraging race for the new little Italian team who nearly achieve their first Championship score. After qualifying 22nd Caffi drives determined race to advance to very impressive sixth, in the points, by lap 36. Up to fifth lap 37 but then slips back due to cracked exhaust pipe. Nevertheless takes team's first finish in eighth place.

57

told. Senna all the way — nursing the car and his tyres, pacing himself and taking extreme care not to let his concentration flag as it had in Monaco — a copy-book drive to win his third consecutive Detroit Grand Prix, his third race of the season and to close the gap between himself and Championship leader Alain Prost to twelve points. And yes it was Prost in second place with the fastest lap once more to emphasise McLaren's total dominance. So what happened to the Ferraris? Very bad luck that's what. A frustrated Berger out of third place, after he'd been passed by Prost, with a puncture caused by a nudge from Boutsen's Benetton and the jinxed Alboreto punted into a spin by Nannini's nearly brakeless Benetton when he was fourth. Michele fought back from last but one to seventh with a fine drive only to spin out of contention of his own volition on lap 46.

With Boutsen a solid third from lap eight the racing was behind him although sadly the retirement list at Detroit embraced over two-thirds of the entry. The Judd-powered cars all fell out with engine-related problems (but not all actually to do with John Judd's hardware) — the two Williams of Mansell and Patrese from fighting fourth places, Gugelmin's March from an excellent fifth and the Ligiers of Arnoux and Johansson after another wasted journey. Nelson Piquet didn't have engine trouble though. With Honda power you wouldn't expect him to. He spun out of the race from an unimpressive ninth place on lap 23, and, at Detroit, was probably not too sorry it was over for him.

But four men covered themselves and their teams with glory. Andrea De Cesaris had one of his 'on' days and magnificently fought his way up to fourth in his new-for-'88 Rial and stayed there from lap 27. Jonathan Palmer, after a pit stop on lap one to change a collision-damaged front wing, tigered from last to fifth in his Tyrrell making, as he did so, the eighth-fastest lap of the race to finish in the points for the third time in six races — a great drive. Alex Caffi drove a fast and sensible race to eighth place to confirm his ability and give the new Dallara team its first

Wherever he goes Ayrton's Brazilian fans are there.

Race 6 — USA EAST

GP finish. But more noteworthy even than those three outstanding drives was that of Pierluigi Martini the little Italian who had replaced the found-wanting Adrian Campos in the Minardi team and who drove an absolute storm of a race. After determinedly working his way up from 18th he held fifth place for fifteen laps and finally finished sixth after being passed by the charging Jonathan Palmer — a drive which, like that of De Cesaris, gave his team its first ever World Championship point.

With only nine drivers classified as finishers and only Senna and Prost going the full distance hardly a sensational race. But it was one which showed that the little teams — Dallara, Rial, Minardi and AGS (for Streiff not only caught Piquet in the early stages of the race but passed him to seventh before having to retire) could do well when the conditions were right for them. As they had been at Detroit.

But now the fast circuits were coming — France, Silverstone and Germany. At them the turbos would be even more dominant and if McLaren could win so convincingly on the twists and turns of Detroit they would hardly be likely to lose when they could really stretch their Honda legs.

Alliot's high-wire act almost puts De Cesaris in the shade.

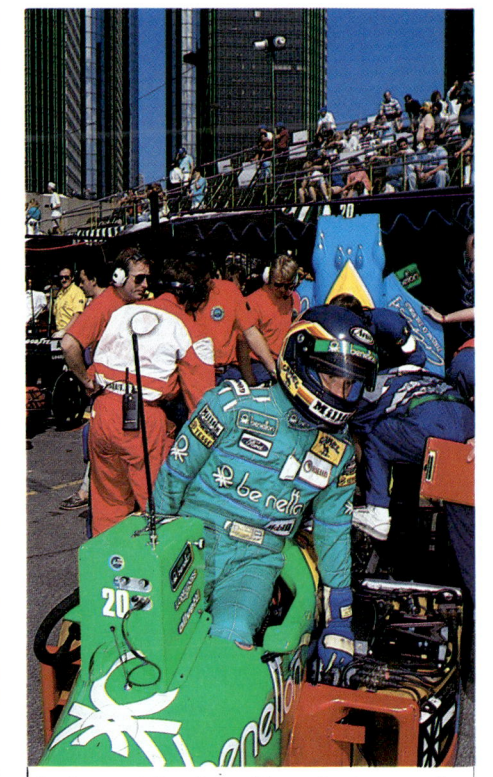

Boutsen and Benetton a blaze of colour — a fine third place was the reward.

59

MURRAY WALKER'S GRAND PRIX YEAR

High rise blocks — low lying Williams.

USA EAST GRAND PRIX

Winner: Ayrton Senna, McLaren-Honda MP4/4-02　　**Fastest Lap:** Alain Prost, 85.848 mph

GRID POSITION		RESULTS			WORLD CHAMPIONSHIP			
No	Driver	Pos. Driver	Car	Drivers		Pts	Constructors	Pts
12	Senna	1 Senna	McLaren-Honda MP4/4-02	1.	Prost	45	1. McLaren-Honda	78
28	Berger	2 Prost	McLaren-Honda MP4/4-04	2.	Senna	33	2. Ferrari	27
27	Alboreto	3 Boutsen	Benetton-Ford B188-05	3.	Berger	18	3. Lotus-Honda	12
11	Prost	4 De Cesaris	Rial-Cosworth ARC1/02	4.	Boutsen	11	Benetton-Ford	12
20	Boutsen	5 Palmer	Tyrrell-Cosworth DG/017-1		Piquet	11	5. Arrows-Megatron	9
5	Mansell	6 Martini	Minardi-Cosworth M188-01	6.	Alboreto	9	6. Tyrrell-Cosworth	5
19	Nannini	7 Dalmas	Lola-Cosworth LC88-01	7.	Warwick	8	7. Rial-Cosworth	3
1	Piquet	8 Caffi	Dallara-Cosworth F188/001	8.	Palmer	5	8. March-Judd	2
17	Warwick	9 Bailey	Tyrrell-Cosworth DG/017-2	9.	De Cesaris	3	9. Williams-Judd	1
6	Patrese			10.	Capelli	2	Minardi-Cosworth	1
14	Streiff			11.	Cheever	1		
22	De Cesaris				Martini	1		
15	Gugelmin				Nakajima	1		
30	Alliot				Nannini	1		
18	Cheever				Patrese	1		
23	Martini							
3	Palmer							
26	Johansson							
33	Modena							
25	Arnoux							
36	Caffi							
4	Bailey							
32	Larrauri							
29	Dalmas							
24	Sala							
21	Larini							

3rd July 1988
Circuit: Paul Ricard

France

WHEN Alain Prost arrived at Le Castellet for the French Grand Prix he may have been leading the World Championship but he did so with the knowledge that, because it is awarded to the driver with the best eleven out of sixteen scores, he was no better off than Senna who, like him, had won three of the first six events. So in a situation where one of the McLaren drivers looked certain to win on the Paul Ricard circuit a fourth victory was of great importance to both of them. Senna had beaten Prost in the last two races but when I talked to Alain about Round Seven he was, as ever, totally relaxed and cheerful. 'I'm delighted to be in the lead and especially to have got six points at Detroit which I hate. But for me this is where the Championship starts. It is good to be back in Europe. This is France. I am a Frenchman and I want to win!'

His friends in the Grand Prix world see Alain as a friendly, cheerful, enormously likeable and very professional man but when you are in France you very quickly realise that he is far more than that to his countrymen. He is certainly one of France's top personalities. You constantly see him on TV, in the press, on posters — everywhere — and in terms of motivation the support and adulation he gets wherever he goes, must have been worth a second a lap to him at Paul Ricard! That's how it seemed during the Friday and Saturday qualifying sessions anyway, for he did something he hadn't done since Monaco 1986 — took pole position. Which not only helped in the discreet psychological war being conducted between Senna and himself but also denied the Brazilian what would have been a record seventh successive first place on the grid.

With the two McLarens in their customary grid positions their symmetry was continued in the next three rows — two Ferraris, two Benettons and two Lotuses driven by Berger, Alboreto, Boutsen, Nannini, Piquet and Nakajima. Which was a real achievement by the two Benetton drivers for the circuit certainly did not favour their normally aspirated Ford-engined cars. The Circuit Paul Ricard is situated on a rocky plateau at an altitude of some 2,000 feet which, in conjunction with the high temperatures we were all enjoying, meant that they were some fifty horsepower down on their usual

I know it's France René, but you can't do it there!

61

power output. A problem which did not affect the turbocar drivers who were able to exploit their full 650 horsepower — especially down the long 195 miles an hour Mistral Straight. With less than a second separating the next nine cars headed by the Williams-Judd of Nigel Mansell (who had won the French GP in 1986 and '87 but who'd got about as much chance of making it three in a row as he had of winning Wimbledon) it looked as though we were in for an interesting event. And it was!

For the first time in seven races we had a genuine battle for the lead between the two top men in the top car — Prost and Senna. For one reason or another we'd been denied this at Brazil, San Marino, Monaco, Mexico, Canada and Detroit but in France it happened. An ultra-confident Prost took the lead as the race began and by the end of the second lap he was some one and a half seconds ahead of Senna who had Berger's Ferrari right behind him followed by Alboreto, Piquet, Boutsen, Nannini and Mansell. The McLarens were in no danger from anyone else but they were certainly a danger to themselves for the blistering pace they were setting was eating into their fuel in a way that was later to cause concern to the Honda technicians monitoring their consumption from the pitlane. Prost, happy with the way the race was going, kept a two second cushion between himself and Senna which, try as Ayrton may, he could do nothing to reduce. In fact on lap 34 the gap increased to 22 seconds when Senna dived into the pits for a new set of Goodyears. In recent races we'd got used to the entire distance being done on one set of 'boots' but there was no question of this at Paul Ricard whose abrasive surface demanded a stop for new rubber. So three laps later in came Alain for what turned out to be a longer stop than Senna's and which resulted in him rejoining the race about three seconds behind his colleague. Now they were both in very heavy traffic lapping their rivals — a situation where Senna usually does better than Prost. But not this time. Driving coolly, precisely and very forcefully Alain sliced his way through the backmarkers and closed the gap to nothing. On the 45th circuit he made the fastest lap of the day (one minute 11.737 seconds = 118.85 mph, 1.9 seconds slower than Nigel Mansell's 1987 record) and on lap 60 in an absolutely breathtaking manoeuvre he dived inside Senna at the daunting 190 mph Courbe de Signes corner to retake the lead he had lost 23 laps before. A lead he never lost for now Senna was wrestling with a spongy gear linkage which completely destroyed his race rhythm. That, coupled with the need for both of them to conserve fuel, maintained the status quo and gave Prost his 32nd Grand Prix victory, and much more importantly to him, his fourth win of 1988 which established his genuine Championship leadership. And Senna? Very generous in defeat. 'It was Alain's day. I did my best but it was not good enough. With the equal cars and team backing that we have got, I look forward to many more battles like today's in the races that remain.' So did we!

The Ferrari fight behind the McLarens was good too. After the 'night of the long knives' at Maranello John Barnard had emerged victorious and Harvey Postlethwaite was going to Tyrrell — almost immediately. John was at Paul Ricard and very much in charge to the delight of Gerhard Berger, but not of Michele Alboreto who, like Postlethwaite, appeared to be moving on at the end of the season. The cars went well. Not as well as the McLarens but well enough to take third and fourth places for Alboreto (one of Grand Prix racing's Gentlemen) to be the one in front, and on the same lap as Prost and Senna at the finish — in itself a considerable achievement! — was a very pleasing result. It had initially been Berger who held the third place but a spin when he missed a gear on lap 22 let Michele through and subsequently forced him into the pits for an early tyre change. Gerhard retook third place later but his early stop meant that his tyres were rooted later in the race which allowed Alboreto to get past for his second well-earned third place of 1988.

World Champion Nelson Piquet continued his disappointing 1988 by running in fifth place for almost the whole race. He may have been out-qualified by the Benettons but the greater power and improved handling of his Lotus-Honda (fitted with some trick electronically-controlled Bilstein shock

Race 7 — FRANCE

Wearing four other people's overalls, Yannick Dalmas found his car and finished 13th.

Red and blue shoes and a black and blue foot — Ivan Capelli lucky to be in France after his Detroit crash.

Entente cordiale! Nigel Mansell and Isabelle Magnillat, FISA's super press officer.

TEAM ANALYSIS

LOTUS
Amidst disturbing rumours about Lotus racing future (suggested 1989 loss of Sponsor, Team Manager, Designer, Honda engine and drivers) Team has mediocre time in France. With revised aerodynamics and special electronically-controlled Bilstein shock absorbers Piquet and Nakajima qualify only seventh and eighth. Piquet races and finishes fifth (one lap down) with stripped second gear and clutch problem. Nakajima takes seventh place with broken gear selector.

TYRRELL
Ken Tyrrell announces that Ferrari top technician Harvey Postlethwaite joins his Team in August to design new 1989 car at newly built factory. Jonathan Palmer starts 24th, improves to 16th by lap 29 but pulls out with failing engine on lap 41. At first Paul Ricard GP appearance Julian Bailey fails to qualify.

WILLIAMS
Previous engine overheating seemingly corrected by bigger radiators and revised plumbing but other problems mar race after Mansell qualifies ninth and Patrese 15th. Mansell races seventh/eighth behind Nannini's Benetton with fading power until broken rear suspension wishbone causes lap 33 retirement from ninth place after tyre stop. With seven retirements from as many races Mansell rumoured to be moving to Ferrari in 1989. Patrese retires from 21st on lap 36 with brake problems caused by balance control failure. Only two finishes from fourteen starts for Williams team so far.

ZAKSPEED
A much troubled team with second rate car/engine/driver package. Ghinzani qualifies 22nd but excluded from race for failing to stop for weight check in Saturday practice. Schneider starts 21st for his second GP. Races at rear of field until lap 55 retirement with broken gearbox.

McLAREN
Where others falter and fail McLaren again demonstrate total superiority. On home ground Prost takes his first pole position of 1988, wins his fourth race of the year, makes fastest lap and increases World Championship lead over Senna with a faultless drive. Senna almost as impressive with fine drive to second place from second on grid hampered by 'spongy' gear selectors. McLaren now lead Constructors' Championship by 59 points!

AGS
With a Heini Mader Ford DFZ engine modified for special ELF fuel, Phillipe Streiff qualifies 17th but after improving to fifteenth has to retire on lap 17 due to fuel from split cell causing painful leg burns.

MARCH
An excellent French GP for the ever-improving Bicester team. With revised 'anti-dive' front suspension Ivan Capelli qualifies very well at tenth despite having left foot in a cast following Detroit GP crash. After racelong battles against Cheever, De Cesaris and Caffi finishes ninth (one lap down). Gugelmin has best GP yet starting 16th and fighting up to finish eighth (one lap down) with no clutch for last 25 laps.

Pretty car. Pity about the drive — Derek crashed on lap 12.

ARROWS
In spite of 'better' Megatron engines, Warwick and Cheever qualify disappointingly low on 'turbo' circuit or eleventh (Warwick) and thirteenth. Warwick still experiencing breathing problems and muscle pain after Canada crash. The closely matched pair have their usual race battle — this time for the tenth place — until Warwick spins heavily into pit wall avoiding gear-fumbling Nakajima on lap twelve. Cheever improves to sixth by lap 35 but, with acute oversteer, subsequently slides back to finish eleventh (two laps down).

BENETTON
Benetton consolidate their position as the best of the 3½ litre teams with excellent fifth and sixth positions on the grid for Boutsen and Nannini — ahead of Piquet Lotus and six other turbo cars. Boutsen holds sixth place for sixteen laps before dropping back to rear of field and retiring after 28 laps with electrical problems. Drops two places to sixth in Championship. Nannini drives excellent race to finish sixth for third time in 1988 and top NA (one lap down). Team down one place to fourth in Constructors' Championship (top NA).

Race 7 — FRANCE

Gugelmin — his March in the sun brought eighth place.

OSELLA
Larini qualifies 24th for his third GP of 1988. Races at rear of field until lap 57 when retires with broken drive-shaft.

RIAL
Gunther Schmidt's RIAL team continues to perform consistently better than his previous ATS equipe. De Cesaris twelfth on grid for the fourth time. Finishes tenth in race (one lap down) after long battle with Capelli, Cheever and Caffi and despite overlong pit stop with faulty wheel air-wrench.

MINARDI
For his second 1988 GP Pierluigi Martini qualifies 23rd before racing to last classified fifteenth place, three laps down after losing time due to delaying tyre change. Luis Perez-Sala qualifies last at 26th. Progresses to 18th, lap 29, before losing ten laps with plug/coil problems. Not classified as finisher.

LIGIER
In what is turning out to be Ligier's worst season ever both Arnoux and Johansson fail to qualify. Car needs far more than the minor changes which can be made during the hectic Grand Prix season.

FERRARI
Technical Director John Barnard appears at Le Castellet with greatly enhanced power following the Maranello 'palace revolution' which, amongst other things, sees the departure of top technician Harvey Postlethwaite to Tyrrell. Now seems likely that Barnard-designed 3½ litre V12 car will race before season's end. At Paul Ricard Berger and Alboreto qualify third and fourth and nearer to McLarens than before. Then race behind Prost/Senna to third (Alboreto) and fourth with Alboreto on same lap as the McLaren men — quite an achievement these days!

LOLA
Closely matched Alliot and Dalmas qualify 18th and 19th. After initially dropping back to 23rd Dalmas moves up to finish 13th (two laps down). Alliot, in another determined race, improves to twelfth, lap 33, but subsequently retires, lap 47, with engine management system problems.

COLONI
For the second race in succession Tarquini fails to pre-qualify during Friday morning practice.

EUROBRUN
Modena qualifies 20th and, by virtue of good steady race, finishes 14th (three laps down). Larrauri, 27th fastest in practice, fails to qualify but starts 26th on grid after Ghinzani exclusion. Races at rear of field until lap 65 retirement (clutch).

DALLARA
Another stout effort by Alex Caffi who qualifies 14th, spends most of the race in the company of De Cesaris and finishes twelfth (two laps down).

65

MURRAY WALKER'S GRAND PRIX YEAR

Bouygues build roads — Streiff certainly needed one.

Race 7 — FRANCE

absorbers for the first time) enabled him to keep ahead of them during the race in spite of the fact that he had no second gear during the final fifteen laps. Once again though the multi-coloured Benettons were the class of the 3½ litre field. Thierry Boutsen, who had been looking a bit outclassed by Alessandro Nannini in recent races, was the top man in the team this time with an excellent drive in sixth place behind Nelson Piquet until lap 17 when a variety of electrical problems sidelined him for his first retirement of the season. Boutsen's misfortune was to Nannini's advantage, however, for he inherited the sixth place that Thierry had lost to score his third championship point of the year.

As in every Grand Prix there were winners and losers and this time the tremendously enthusiastic and ebullient March team were amongst the winners. Both Mauricio Gugelmin and Ivan Capelli drove excellent races to take eighth and ninth places in their Judd-powered cars which was not only of considerable encouragement to them but also to John Judd whose first season of Grand Prix racing with the Williams, Ligier and March teams was turning out to be a character-building experience! Capelli's drive was a very real achievement for he raced with his fractured left foot in a slipper cast after his Detroit crash only two weeks earlier. His Team Manager Ian Phillips who was present when Ivan was given his fitness-to-drive medical said that his fixed grin and protestations that 'it doesn't hurt at all Doctor' whilst his foot was being agonisingly twisted this way and that more than repaid all the practical jokes he had suffered at 'Dustin's' hands! (Capelli is Hoffman's double.)

So March were winners but once again the Williams team were losers. With revised plumbing and bigger radiators they appeared to have overcome their engine cooling problems but a thoroughly disillusioned Nigel Mansell had his seventh successive retirement when his rear suspension gave up and removed him from a hard-fought eighth place. The rumours that he had already signed for Ferrari seemed likely to be confirmed at a Press conference he had called at Silverstone the next week. Patrese too retired — on lap 36 with locking brakes.

With no rear wheels, Gerhard did well to finish fourth!

With fifteen classified finishers out of the twenty-six starters the French Grand Prix had provided some excellent entertainment in glorious Cote d'Azur weather. Notably because of the superb all-out driving of Prost and Senna which really kept everyone's eyes fixed at the front of the field. But with the continued dominance of the McLaren team and no sign of anything happening to disrupt it, the inside talk in France was more and more of the build up to 1989. Was Gerhard Berger's 1989 team-mate going to be Nigel Mansell? Was the Camel Sponsorship moving from Lotus to Tyrrell? Was Michele Alboreto joining Ken's team next year? Would the 3½ litre V12 Ferrari be raced this season now that its designer John Barnard had won in the Maranello power struggle? What was going to happen to Lotus who were rumoured to have major Sponsor, Team Manager, Designer, engine supplier and driver problems?

In comparison with the French Grand Prix at Paul Ricard the *Dallas* soap opera was a kids' tea party!

France's hero Alain Prost — his third French Grand Prix victory was one of his best.

FRENCH GRAND PRIX

Winner: Alain Prost, McLaren-Honda MP4/4-04   Fastest Lap: Alain Prost, 118.898 mph

GRID POSITION		RESULTS			WORLD CHAMPIONSHIP			
No.	Driver	Pos. Driver	Car	Drivers	Pts	Constructors	Pts
11	Prost	1 Prost	McLaren-Honda MP4/4-04	1. Prost	54	1. McLaren-Honda	93
12	Senna	2 Senna	McLaren-Honda MP4/4-02	2. Senna	39	2. Ferrari	34
28	Berger	3 Alboreto	Ferrari F187/88C-103	3. Berger	21	3. Lotus-Honda	14
27	Alboreto	4 Berger	Ferrari F187/88C-104	4. Alboreto	13	4. Benetton-Ford	13
20	Boutsen	5 Piquet	Lotus-Honda 100T/2	Piquet	13	5. Arrows-Megatron	9
19	Nannini	6 Nannini	Benetton-Ford B188-03	6. Boutsen	11	6. Tyrrell-Cosworth	5
1	Piquet	7 Nakajima	Lotus-Honda 100T/1	7. Warwick	8	7. Rial-Cosworth	3
2	Nakajima	8 Gugelmin	March-Judd 881/3	8. Palmer	5	8. March-Judd	2
5	Mansell	9 Capelli	March-Judd 881/1	9. De Cesaris	3	9. Williams-Judd	1
16	Capelli	10 De Cesaris	Rial-Cosworth ARC1/01	10. Capelli	2	Minardi-Cosworth	1
17	Warwick	11 Cheever	Arrows-Megatron A10B/01	Nannini	2		
22	De Cesaris	12 Caffi	Dallara-Cosworth F188/001	12. Cheever	1		
18	Cheever	13 Dalmas	Lola-Cosworth LC88-03	Martini	1		
36	Caffi	14 Modena	EuroBrun-Cosworth 188-03	Nakajima	1		
6	Patrese	15 Martini	Minardi-Cosworth M188-01	Patrese	1		
15	Gugelmin						
14	Streiff						
30	Alliot						
29	Dalmas						
33	Modena						
10	Schneider						
23	Martini						
3	Palmer						
21	Larini						
24	Sala						
32	Larrauri						

10th July 1988
Circuit: Silverstone

Great Britain

AT Silverstone on 10th July the Grand Prix season came alive. Although the previous seven races had been full of interest to the knowledgeable enthusiast the series had become boring to the vastly greater uncommitted TV audience who were tired of what they saw as dull and repetitive McLaren benefits. But they could hardly believe their eyes as they watched the British Grand Prix action at Silverstone — without doubt the best 1988 race yet. Two Ferraris on the front row of the starting grid! McLarens only third and fourth! Two 3½ litre Marches on row three! A Ferrari leading the race! A revitalised Nigel Mansell charging up the field from eleventh to second, making the fastest lap — and not retiring! Heroic driving at frightening speeds with seemingly nil visibility on a rain-soaked track. Spinning cars. Tyre changes which affected positions. Places lost as drivers ran out of fuel. And only one McLaren finishing — even if it did win. This was indeed different. And they loved it!

For Silverstone's fortieth year the RAC Motor Sports Association, the organisers of the historic British Grand Prix, had made a maximum effort in association with the British Racing Drivers' Club — the owners of the circuit. A magnificent new Press Centre costing over £750,000 greeted the delighted Media Corps. A new internal ring road had been built. Debris fencing inside and out. 30,000 Grandstand seats. Two massive Star Screens to show the BBC TV pictures to spectators at Stowe and Woodcote. 200,000 square feet of tented accommodation for Corporate Hospitality. 3,000 helicopter movements to shift 7,000 people in and out of the circuit — a one-day world record. Five helicopters on circuit stand-by for medical emergencies. So it was indeed tragic that the RAC MSA Chief Executive, the popular Peter Hammond, was killed in a road accident on his way to the track. But a tribute to the organisation that he had headed that it was able to carry the unexpected burden in his very much missed absence.

The Northamptonshire ex-RAF Bomber airfield circuit was very different to the seven 1988 tracks which had preceded it. Their fastest lap record had been Imola's at 127.15 mph. Silverstone's is 153.06! To get the best out of a car on its 195 mph Hangar Straight and its high-speed sweeps and curves with

It's a tight fit in the super-slippery March!

69

no corner needing a gear lower than third, a driver needs lots of top-end power and perfect car balance. Which is exactly what the Ferraris had got but had been unable to utilise fully at the earlier venues. And the result was that on Saturday afternoon the exultant Maranello mechanics were preparing the cars that would be on the front row of the grid next day — with Berger in pole position and Alboreto next to him. No McLaren in the first two places for the first time since Mexico 1987! Why? Because in their usual thoroughgoing leave-no-stone-unturned way the Woking team had made some major alterations to the aerodynamics of their cars to suit the forthcoming high speed Grands Prix (British, German and Italian). New bodywork, revised air inlets and intercoolers — at a reputed cost of some £150,000. All to no avail because they adversely affected the handling of the cars. So they were abandoned after Friday. And with only Saturday to get their cars set up after the previous components had been replaced Senna and Prost were half a second off the pace. Which was enough to lose them those top two places.

But if that was dramatic the Williams story was sensational. Firstly came the news that Nigel Mansell had signed for Ferrari in 1989. Then, after a series of frightening high speed departures from the track on Friday with major handling deficiencies due to aeration of the Reactive suspension system hydraulics a disheartened Mansell was almost in a state of revolt — as was Patrese. With Nigel thirteenth and Riccardo slowest of all at thirtieth Designer Patrick Head took a bold and brave decision — 'abandon it.' In a situation where the FW12 had been designed around the Reactive system and was theoretically unconvertible to conventional springs and shock absorbers there was a major overnight blitz at Didcot to design and fabricate a new system and find the necessary parts. Amazingly they did it and on Saturday after an 'all nighter' by the weary mechanics a delighted Nigel Mansell qualified eleventh in a car he felt he could trust enough to drive in his usual totally

The Ferraris flattered to deceive. First and second at the start but nowhere at the finish.

Race 8 — GREAT BRITAIN

committed ten-tenths way. An astounding demonstration of what human beings can do when the pressure is on.

And further to underline the fact that Silverstone was indeed different the aerodynamic March masterpieces of the talented Adrian Newey were not only fifth and sixth on the grid with Mauricio Gugelmin and Ivan Capelli at their wheels but were the fastest 'atmospheric' cars — faster than the previously dominant Benetton-Fords. So with a new look to the grid and the possibility of the McLaren mould being broken tomorrow the prospects for the half-way Round Eight of the Championship were indeed exciting!

The bad news on Sunday was that the weather was awful. Grey skies and unremitting rain meant that it was going to be the first wet Grand Prix since Portugal 1985. The good news though was that the wet conditions would surely narrow the gap between the turbos and the atmospherics. And they did! Berger's start was good. Senna's was superb. Prost's was awful. By Maggots, the second bend on the track, Senna was tight up behind the Ferrari in second place and even made an unsuccessful try for the lead at Stowe. And at the end of the lap 'atmo' drivers were fourth, fifth, sixth and seventh — Gugelmin, Capelli, Nannini and Mansell. Followed by the World Championship leader Alain Prost languishing in a very unhappy-looking ninth.

On lap three Capelli dropped back with electrical troubles and then for ten laps there was no change as, in truly appalling conditions with their red rear warning lights glowing through thick grey clouds of hanging spray at up to 200 miles an hour, the top six fought it out. The crowd may have been wet and bedraggled but it mattered not. This was real spine-tingling, nerve-jangling top level racing at the limit, far exceeding their expectations.

By lap thirteen Michele Alboreto was fighting to hold his third place with Gugelmin, Nannini and Mansell right behind him whilst ahead, on lap fourteen, Senna the Rainmaster took the lead. At Estoril in the 1985 Portuguese GP he had demonstrated his consummate talent with a first victory drive in conditions which were even worse than today's and here he was doing it again

as he took Berger on the approach to the new left/right after the bridge and lapped his Championship-leading team-mate Alain Prost who was controversially to retire ten laps later with 'dangerous handling'.

'Big Brother' Frank is watching you Pierluigi and Philippe!

Heroes all! Nannini, Capelli and Mansell versus each other and the rain.

Then, with Senna out of the wall of spray and steadily pulling away from the Ferrari, the excited attention of the crowd switched to the battle for third place between Alboreto, Nannini and Mansell. What a battle it was too! Between Stowe and Club on lap twenty Mansell, with a mixture of skill, experience and sheer bravery passed Alessandro Nannini to fourth at which the Italian spun andlet Gugelmin through to

71

TEAM ANALYSIS

LOTUS
Only a mediocre British Grand Prix for Lotus. Seventh and tenth on the grid for Piquet and Nakajima. With Honda turbo power Piquet drives reliable but unimpressive full-distance race to finish fifth behind Senna's McLaren and three NA cars. Retains fourth in Championship. Nakajima has long battle with Warwick, Cheever and Patrese until loses second gear in eighth place on lap 50. Finishes tenth. Team down to fourth in Constructors' Championship.

TYRRELL
Coincidental with imminent arrival of Harvey Postlethwaite Design Engineer Maurice Phillipe announces departure from team. In car which is definitely not a 3½ litre front runner Palmer qualifies 17th and Bailey 24th at a circuit both know well. After engine problem on parade lap Palmer starts from pit lane. Runs last with motor problem for 14 laps before retirement. With lack of grip Bailey races towards rear of field for first real GP finish in 16th place (two laps down).

WILLIAMS
After continued major problems with Reactive suspension in Friday practice Designer Patrick Head makes dramatic decision to shelve it. High pressure overnight design and fabrication work at Didcot incredibly results in conventional 'springs and shockers' appearing on Mansell car on Saturday — to his great relief. Despite strange new set up Nigel qualifies eleventh. With mind at ease, then drives quite brilliant race in appalling conditions to an inspired second for first 1988 finish with fastest lap (one minute 23.31 seconds = 128.3 mph — thirteen seconds slower than own dry-track 1987 record). Resultant six points for best 1988 NA finish so far takes him straight to eighth and Williams to sixth in their respective Championships. Patrese qualifies 15th with Reactive suspension. Then races to praiseworthy eighth (one lap down) with unknown conventional set up. Team will now continue with obviously superior normal suspension until Reactive perfected by R & D. 'Thank God for that,' say the drivers! Mansell confirms his move to Ferrari in 1989.

ZAKSPEED
Eric Zakowski's Team's eminently forgettable season continues its depressing way with both Ghinzani and Schneider failing to qualify due to poor handling and lack of grunt at 'power' circuit.

Even with Honda turbo-power, Nelson only finished fifth.

McLAREN
Team Perfect gets it wrong for once. At vast expense McLaren adopt new 'fast circuit' turbo inlets and intercooler set up to improve aerodynamics. Resultant balance problems adversely affect performance so both Prost and Senna behind Ferraris in Friday qualifying. Saturday return to previous set-up leaves insufficient time to balance cars. Senna/Prost third and fourth on grid — first time no McLaren on front row since Mexico 1987. Nevertheless brilliant drive gives Senna fourth 1988 win to close within six points of Prost in Championship. After bad start Prost fails to finish for first time in 1988 when controversially retires from 16th place with evil handling, lap 25. Nevertheless Team lead in Constructors' Championship now up to 68 points.

AGS
Streiff, recovered from French GP fuel burns, starts 16th to be immediately rammed by Sala's Minardi. Retires from 20th place, lap nine, with broken rear wing.

MARCH
Best GP yet for March! Super-slippery Adrian Newey design, further helped by new front suspension and higher compression Judd engine, proves to be superb at full-bore Silverstone. Gugelmin and Capelli magnificently occupy row three of grid — fifth and sixth and fastest NA cars. On first GP circuit he is really familiar with Gugelmin drives superb race to go full distance and finish fourth — in points for first time and passed only by Mansell and Nannini. After improving to fifth Capelli retires from ninth, lap 34, with alternator problems.

Mauricio Gugelmin's first points. A superb drive in the stunning March-Judd.

Race 8 — GREAT BRITAIN

ARROWS
Warwick qualifies ninth. Cheever 13th. Strong race by both drivers with stirring finish when they pass Berger on last corner to take sixth (Warwick) and seventh places (one lap down) separated by only seven-tenths of second. Warwick remains seventh in Championship.

BENETTON
Success for Nannini. Failure for Boutsen (who announces he will drive for Williams in 1989). Nannini starts eighth but fights up to superb third for first podium finish in spite of two spins caused by faulty brake balance when battling with inspired Mansell. ('I adjusted it when I passed him,' says Nigel!) With car balance problems at a circuit where perfection is essential Boutsen qualifies only twelfth. Retires from eighth place, lap 29, when engine blows causing minor oil fire. Team improves to third in Constructors' Championship.

OSELLA
Larini just qualifies at 26th. Races towards rear of field until lap 61 when runs out of fuel. Nevertheless takes last classified place at 19th (five laps down).

RIAL
De Cesaris qualifies 14th. Retires from 20th place, lap nine, with broken clutch plate.

MINARDI
During Friday qualifying session Martini destroys race car. Qualifies 19th in spare. Races to 15th (two laps down) with acute oversteer. Sala rams Streiff lap one and retires immediately with deranged nosecone, broken right front suspension and black mark.

LIGIER
Despite seemingly endless aerodynamic and suspension experimentation novel car no better at Silverstone than previous seven circuits. Arnoux qualifies 25th. Grittily improves to 19th lap one but then drops to last, laps 34 to 62, to finish 18th (three laps down). Johansson tries to qualify new chassis but fails. Williams team aerodynamicist Frank Dernie said to be joining Ligier in 1989. They certainly need him.

FERRARI
The Commendatore's well balanced car with strong top-end power well suited to Silverstone. Berger (pole) and Alboreto displace Senna and Prost from front row of grid for first time in 1988. Berger leads until lap 14. Second to Senna laps 14-49. Then, obliged to save fuel, eases off to slide down and finish ninth with dry tank (losing three places on the last corner!). Alboreto runs third laps 1-21. As weather changes, stops twice for new tyres — first for slicks and then back to wets. Runs out of fuel on lap 62 but classified 17th (three laps down).

LOLA
In straightforward but disappointing meeting the closely matched Alliot and Dalmas qualify 22nd and 23rd. Equally well matched in race they finish 13th (Dalmas) and 14th nine seconds apart with 'no grip' (both two laps down).

COLONI
Although the unfortunate Gabriele Tarquini finishes Friday morning's free practice in 26th place ahead of five other drivers he is excluded from further participation in view of the fact that they all drive for 'Pre-1988' full-season teams and therefore take precedence.

EUROBRUN
Larrauri again fails to qualify. Modena starts 20th. By virtue of good steady drive and retirements ahead finishes well at 12th only one lap down.

DALLARA
In a car vastly superior to the Osella he drove in 1987 Caffi continues to underline the class he has been showing in 1988 by racing to finish eleventh (one lap down) from his grid position of 21st.

Express? Only the Ferrari — Stefan Johansson didn't qualify.

MURRAY WALKER'S GRAND PRIX YEAR

Rainmaster Senna wins the race . . .

Inspired Mansell wins the crowd . . .

74

Race 8 — GREAT BRITAIN

Dejected Berger wins nothing.

fifth! (In his long battle with Mansell Sandro was to spin again later but got away with it both times.)

Two laps later at exactly the same place Nigel was third, past Alboreto's Ferrari turbo in the car which until then had been sadly regarded as a travesty of its Championship winning predecessors. It is difficult for me to find the right words to describe Nigel's drive but it was certainly one of the greatest I've seen in my forty years of commentating. Seeking out wet patches to cool his tyres as the track dried he drove with controlled ferocity never putting a wheel wrong. As he wondrously cut deep into the big lead that the second-placed Gerhard Berger had over him he made the fastest lap of the race. Faster than Senna. Faster than Berger. Faster than Alboreto. Faster than all the other 3½ litres. One minute 23.308 seconds. An average of 128.3 miles an hour. In those conditions! And on lap fifty with fifteen to go, to explosions of sheer delight from the programme-waving, shouting and cheering crowd he passed Berger to second evoking memories of his breathtaking move to first past Piquet the previous year. Oh God please don't let him break down now!

He didn't. With the sturdy V8 Judd behind him never missing a beat — to uplift its unjustifiably tarnished reputation — he finished only 23 seconds behind Senna having considerably more than halved the gap that had once existed between them. Sheer Tiger! But there was more to come in this enthralling race. With Alboreto long since out of the picture as a result of changing to slick tyres when the conditions improved only to have to return for wets when it rained again Berger was sliding backwards with a massive fuel deficit. Past him went Nannini to third, then Gugelmin to fourth and Piquet to fifth. And on the very last corner with the Chequered Flag in sight Warwick, Cheever and Patrese to sixth, seventh and eighth! Poor Gerhard. And poor Ferrari. No points again after such a promising start.

So with a stunning drive Senna made it four wins from eight races to equal Prost's record and reduce Alain's Championship lead to a slim six points. After the race people were criticising Prost for pulling out and he admitted that his action might well

75

have cost him the World Championship. 'But it's my life,' he said, 'and I didn't see any point in risking it for a mid-field place.' The critics should try sitting in his place! But good as Senna had been the Man of the Day for me was Nigel Mansell with a drive of awesome brilliance in a car which could now obviously see him in the top six in the remaining eight races — and maybe even a win at somewhere slower and twistier like Hungary, Spain or Australia? But as they sat for hours waiting to get out of the sodden car parks the wet but contented thousands who'd watched a great race talked not only of Mansell but of Nannini who, by finishing an excellent third, stood on a Grand Prix podium for the first time. And of the charming newcomer Mauricio Gugelmin who'd earned his first World Championship points with a fighting fourth place that had seen him passed by only two men — Mansell and Nannini.

An enthralling race in which nineteen of the 26 starters finished with the first five on the same lap. 'Let's have some more like that' they said!

And they say that Ron Dennis can't smile!

BRITISH GRAND PRIX

Winner: Ayrton Senna, McLaren-Honda MP4/4-05   *Fastest Lap:* Nigel Mansell, 128.300 mph

GRID POSITION			RESULTS			WORLD CHAMPIONSHIP			
No.	Driver	Pos.	Driver	Car	Drivers	Pts	Constructors		Pts
28	Berger	1	Senna	McLaren-Honda MP4/4-05	1. Prost	54	1. McLaren-Honda		102
27	Alboreto	2	Mansell	Williams-Judd FW12/1	2. Senna	48	2. Ferrari		34
12	Senna	3	Nannini	Benetton-Ford B188-03	3. Berger	21	3. Benetton-Ford		17
11	Prost	4	Gugelmin	March-Judd 881/2	4. Piquet	15	Lotus-Honda		16
15	Gugelmin	5	Piquet	Lotus-Honda 100T/3	5. Alboreto	13	5. Arrows-Megatron		10
16	Capelli	6	Warwick	Arrows-Megatron A10B/03	6. Boutsen	11	6. Williams-Judd		7
1	Piquet	7	Cheever	Arrows-Megatron A10B/01	7. Warwick	9	7. Tyrrell-Cosworth		5
19	Nannini	8	Patrese	Williams-Judd FW12/3	8. Nannini	6	March-Judd		5
17	Warwick	9	Berger	Ferrari F187/88C-104	Mansell	6	9. Rial-Cosworth		3
2	Nakajima	10	Nakajima	Lotus-Honda 100T/1	10. Palmer	5	10. Minardi-Cosworth		1
5	Mansell	11	Caffi	Dallara-Cosworth F188/001	11. De Cesaris	3			
20	Boutsen	12	Modena	EuroBrun-Cosworth 188-03	Gugelmin	3			
18	Cheever	13	Dalmas	Lola-Cosworth LC88-03	13. Capelli	2			
22	De Cesaris	14	Alliot	Lola-Cosworth LC88-04	14. Cheever	1			
6	Patrese	15	Martini	Minardi-Cosworth M188-01	Martini	1			
14	Streiff	16	Bailey	Tyrrell-Cosworth DG/017-3	Nakajima	1			
3	Palmer	17	Alboreto	Ferrari F187/88C-104	Patrese	1			
24	Sala	18	Arnoux	Ligier-Judd JS31/02					
23	Martini	19	Larini	Osella-Alfa FA1L/1					
33	Modena								
36	Caffi								
30	Alliot								
29	Dalmas								
4	Bailey								
25	Arnoux								
21	Larini								

24th July 1988
Circuit: Hockenheim

Germany

ROUND Nine of the World Championship and the start of the second half of the sixteen race series. At the Hockenheimring near the beautiful and historic city of Heidelberg. Not the world's most exciting circuit. Flat, featureless and fast, most of it comprises two long, roughly parallel, curved flat-out legs, each with an artificial chicane to slow things down a bit, which slice through seemingly impenetrable gloomy pine forest. They're joined at the top by the fourth gear Ost Curve with another chicane in it and at the bottom by the seven-bend convoluted 'Stadium' section which is overlooked by an enormous, virtually continuous, concrete grandstand.

At Hockenheim pure speed is the name of the game. With a 143.8 mph lap record (Nigel Mansell/Williams-Honda 1987) it has to be. So you set the car up with the minimum amount of wing and, therefore, downforce, and put up with it sliding about in the Stadium. If the drivers don't like it at least the crowd does! This year while the teams were experimenting with different wings, different ride heights, different spring strengths and a profusion of aerodynamic tweaks (with McLaren quietly relieved to know that here the special bodywork they'd had to abandon at Silverstone was 100% effective) the media men were frantically trying to breathe some excitement into what had become a pretty predictable scene. For, the scenario went, the McLarens were bound to be up front again weren't they? With the Ferraris next if their fuel held out. And then the Benettons — or maybe the Marches or Williams after the way they'd gone at Silverstone. With Piquet's Lotus-Honda in amongst the 3½ litre runners somewhere of course.

But if the race seemed predictable there

The German's lesson — Senna the Ringmeister shows Schneider how to do it.

were always the 'silly season' rumours and counter rumours to gossip about! They seem to start earlier every year and were in full flight at Hockenheim. Mansell to Ferrari and Boutsen to Williams were facts rather than rumours of course and we knew that Harvey Postlethwaite would be designing the 1989 Tyrrell. It seemed very likely that the Williams Team Aerodynamicist and Reactive Suspension designer Frank Dernie was going to Ligier for 'a vast bag of gold'. 'And Martin Brundle's going to be back you know' they said (and wouldn't it be nice if he was). Alboreto was tipped to be leading a two-car Dallara team, and Gustav Brunner was definitely going to draw the next Zakspeed. There were going to be at least 38 cars trying to get into the 1989 Grands Prix season. And very soon the Mercedes Board was going to decide whether to re-enter the scene that they had dominated three times before. 'And forget the story about Lotus being in trouble — they've secured the backing they need and they're talking to Porsche about engines.' True? False? Time would tell and there were undoubtedly even juicier possibilities to come!

For now though just enjoy the weather. Because it was sunny and hot. Very hot. Over 100 degrees. Which is nice. But also humid — which isn't. But at least everybody was able to get their cars set up for the tricky circuit in consistent conditions. Nice and stiff to maintain the minimum ride height and very slippery to maximise the straight line speed. Just what those McLaren mods were designed to do and they did it. Senna was fastest in all five sessions to take his seventh pole position of the year with, of course, Alain Prost alongside him. Then to no one's surprise, it was indeed the two Ferraris next with Berger third 1½ seconds slower than Senna and a second faster than Alboreto. On a fast circuit like Hockenheim you'd expect Piquet to be in the top six. And he was. Fifth. Followed by the now expected Nannini in his 3½ litre Benetton — the fastest normally-aspirated car. And sure enough the Marches were up there too — their immaculate aerodynamics, ideally

The Pathfinders — tail lights guide the way.

Race 9 — GERMANY

suited to the fast going, enabled Capelli to start seventh and Gugelmin tenth with Nakajima and Boutsen between them, and Mansell's Williams-Judd eleventh.

On Saturday night there was a storm like few of us had experienced before. Megavolt lightning flashes, fusilade after fusilade of ear-splitting thunderclaps and torrential rain which led to a Sunday that was heavily overcast and obviously threatening more rain. The carefully contrived dry weather set-ups were right for the dry final half hour of practice on Sunday morning with Gugelmin and Capelli fourth and fifth to split the Ferraris of Alboreto and Berger but as the 26 cars formed up on the starting grid for the 14.30 start it was wet. With the race officially declared to be 'wet' the teams had to make their tyre choice in the knowledge that it wouldn't be stopped if the conditions changed. Virtually all of them opted to start on wet (treaded) tyres. Which seemed a more than sensible decision at 14.30, for as Senna led into turn one he was followed by a vast grey cloud containing invisible cars.

Derek Warwick said 'I couldn't see a thing and drove by the engine note of the car in front of me!' He was on wet tyres but Piquet, having taken a calculated risk was on slicks. At the Ost Curve he paid the penalty for a wrong decision by aquaplaning sideways into the barrier to severely damage his Lotus and limp back to his pit to retire. As he did so some of us grimly remembered that it was at Hockenheim in similar conditions that, in 1982, Ferrari's Didier Pironi had had the appalling practice accident which had ended his car racing career.

Senna the Rainmaster, led from start to finish and there is really very little one can say about his drive to his fifth victory of the year except that it was perfect — as at Silverstone two weeks earlier, he never put a wheel wrong. Behind him with Berger second and Nannini an inspired third Prost was recovering from another bad start. Third past Nannini on lap eight and to second past Berger four laps later. But by then he was twelve seconds behind Senna and no one — not even Alain — takes that much back from

Prost spun off? I don't believe it! Only in practice though.

TEAM ANALYSIS

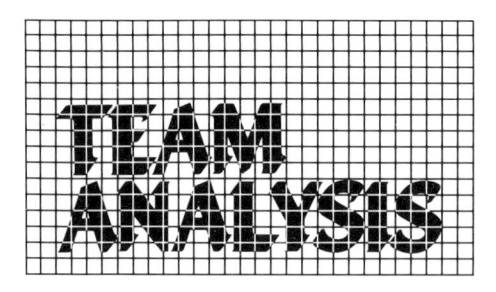

LOTUS
All three team cars fitted with electronically-adjustable Bilstein shock absorbers and 'fast circuit' aerodynamics. For his 150th Grand Prix Piquet qualifies fifth. Makes catastrophic decision to use slick tyres on wet circuit and aquaplanes into chicane barrier on first lap. Withdraws at pit with damaged car. Down to fifth in Championship. Nakajima starts eighth. Runs tenth/twelfth for 34 laps and finishes ninth (one lap down). Team poor fourth in Constructors' Championship.

TYRRELL
In unimpressive car Jonathan Palmer qualifies 24th. Usual determined drive results in eleventh place (one lap down) despite spin on wet track. With 29th fastest practice time Julian Bailey fails to qualify for fifth time. Much needed Harvey Postlethwaite starts as Team's designer on 1st August.

WILLIAMS
A grisly race for Williams with hastily contrived 'Conventional' suspension seen as less than ideal substitute for underdeveloped Reactive system. Mansell a satisfied (under the circumstances) eleventh on the grid. Impressive drive up to seventh by lap eight. Into pit lap 16 with gearbox jammed in fifth. Rejoins after repair but spins out of contention on same lap. After starting 13th Patrese affected by persistent misfire from lap five. Ninth by lap 16 but then spins into retirement lap 35.

ZAKSPEED
Critically important 'home country' race goes well for team. Substantial testing improves engine management system and pop-off valve position. Both drivers qualify — Schneider 22nd and Ghinzani 23rd. Delighted 'German Bernd' achieves first GP finish in twelfth place (one lap down) with 'no problems'. Ghinzani improves to 15th (two laps down) but stops with puncture. Then recovers to finish 14th. With first 1988 double-finish and confirmation of Gustav Brunner as 1989 Technical Director things hopefully looking up for the Niederzissen team.

McLAREN
After successful Hockenheim testing Team uses revised bodywork and intercooler ducting rejected for British GP, to contribute to another memorable weekend. Senna, fastest in all five practice sessions, takes seventh pole of season and faultlessly leads race from start to finish. Prost qualifies second. After bad start fights up from fourth to second on lap twelve. Stays there to retain Championship lead by reduced margin of three points. Unembarrassed Team McLaren now 76 points ahead of Ferrari in Constructors' Championship.

AGS
From sixteenth on grid Streiff decides to risk slick tyres on the wet race track. A bad decision! Stops for wet tyres on lap 19 when nineteenth. Up to 14th lap 35 but retires, lap 38, with broken throttle cable.

Nigel Mansell. Lap 15. No points.

Who is this man? Why hasn't he shaved? What is he trying to say?

Race 9 — GERMANY

MARCH
Another very heartening race for the friendly Bicester team — and for their Judd engine suppliers. Capelli and Gugelmin qualify most impressively at seventh and tenth. Capelli drives superb race to go full distance and finish fifth (first NA driver) despite the early loss of his clutch. On dry settings Gugelmin drops back to 13th lap one but races steadily thereafter to finish eighth (one lap down). Couldn't happen to a nicer team who are now sixth in Constructors' Championship.

ARROWS
After overcoming pop-off valve problems Warwick and Cheever start twelfth and fifteenth (with Cheever inadvertently forcing Berger into terrifying 170 mph 'off' on Saturday). In foul conditions Warwick drives fine but 'thoroughly unpleasant' race to finish seventh after 44 laps pursuit of Boutsen. Cheever has electrical pick-up problem but takes tenth place (one lap down). Team still fifth in Constructors' Championship.

BENETTON
With revised rear suspension to overcome power oversteer Team confirm their 'best NA' rating with Nannini sixth on grid and Boutsen ninth after setting-up problems. Outstanding but heartbreaking race for Nannini. Magnificent third laps 1-8. Fourth laps 9-37. To pit lap 38 with broken throttle cable bracket. After losing four laps rejoins 19th and makes fastest lap of race (two minutes 3.032 seconds = 123.6 mph). Finishes resigned and cheerful 18th. With dry set-up Boutsen fights oversteer, wheelspin and 'no grip' to finish sixth (one lap down). Team retain third place (top NA) in Constructors' Championship.

OSELLA
After rewarding Hockenheim testing Larini qualifies well at 18th. Starts from pit lane on slick tyres. Runs last laps 1-5. In for wet tyres. Retires lap 27 (electrics).

RIAL
Never, a dull moment at Rial! Owner Gunther Schmidt threatens designer Gustav Brunner with lawsuit over association with Zakspeed. De Cesaris paraded before Stewards for doing 120 mph in pit lane! Andrea qualifies 14th in new car with bigger tank. Drives now habitual strong race (including fourth fastest lap) to finish 13th despite two spins, broken wheel and major clutch problem.

MINARDI
After winning the Formula 3000 race at Enna the previous weekend Pierluigi Martini fails to qualify as does Luis Perez-Sala. Both affected by mysterious handling problem.

LIGIER
Following wind tunnel work at St Cyr and Imperial College London Designer Michel Tetu produces 'Qualifying Special' (lightweight monocoque, no rear tank, smaller radiators and high airbox). With revised Judd engine Arnoux uses it to qualify well (for Ligier) at 17th. Thoroughly dispirited Johansson again fails to do so. With usual handling/grip problems Arnoux struggles home to finish 17th (three laps down).

FERRARI
Team again qualify next best to McLaren. Berger third (despite 170 mph spin on Saturday!) and Alboreto fourth. Both drivers again slowed by need to conserve fuel in race. But both go full distance to finish third (Berger) and fourth. For the record Berger and Alboreto third and fourth in Drivers' Championship and Ferrari second in Constructors — but all completely out of touch.

LOLA
Alliot and Dalmas start 20th and 21st. Alliot makes unwise stop for slick tyres on lap nine and then irreparably damages car by sliding into barrier as lapped by Senna on still wet track. Dalmas stops three times with bodywork, tyre and ECU problems but finishes 19th (last classified — five laps down).

Boutsen: 'A touch too much boost there Gerhard!'

COLONI
Despite being 25th fastest out of 31 runners in Friday morning practice the unfortunate Gabriele Tarquini again excluded in line with pre-qualifying rules.

EUROBRUN
Christian Danner unable to take intended place of unimpressive Oscar Larrauri as too tall to fit in car! Modena and Larrauri qualify 25th and 26th. Larrauri crashes in Sunday warm up but takes second GP finish in 16th place. Modena rockets up to 16th lap one. To pit lap six and then retires from last, lap 16, with defective engine.

DALLARA
Caffi 19th on grid. Starts on slick tyres. Races to 15th (two laps down) despite having to drive almost full lap to pit with tyreless right rear wheel after high speed puncture.

81

Another Goodyear for Caffi — urgently needed.

'You hold it and I'll stamp on it,' Nigel Mansell tests revised Williams suspension.

Ayrton. Indeed with traffic problems and then a spin through pressing too hard Prost dropped further back until Senna, slowing in the final laps, allowed the gap to come down to the thirteen seconds it was at the finish. Another One/Two for the invincible McLaren men — their sixth from nine races.

But neither of them put up the fastest lap. That honour went to the gifted Alessandro Nannini in his Benetton-Ford. With a blinding start he shot into third place from sixth on the grid and held it for seven laps until he was passed by 'Superman' Prost. But then he held fourth place ahead of Alboreto until lap 38 of the race's 44 when he was forced into his pit to have a broken throttle bracket (of all things) repaired. After losing four laps he rejoined in last position but one, to drive as though he was going for first, and on lap forty he went round in two minutes 3.032 seconds — a speed of some 123.6 mph and in a 3½ litre car. He finished eighteenth but he'd more than made his mark.

Five men went the distance in the German Grand Prix and nineteen were classified as finishers — both high figures these days. With Berger third and Alboreto fourth both hampered, as they had been at Silverstone, by excessive fuel consumption. Ivan Capelli covered the full forty-four laps to take fifth place (as he had in Canada) in his March-Judd, despite losing his clutch on lap 14 and was actually closing on Alboreto in the closing stages as the Italian cautiously watched his fuel counter. A very fine drive that reflected credit on him, his team and his Judd engine. John Judd had been taking a lot of stick including threatening letters from Mansell 'fans' but the last two races showed that the problems had been more to do with installation than the engine itself.

So what of the other twenty-one starters? Another point for Boutsen for his sixth place (lapped) after fighting a car set up for the dry which behaved as though it was on ice. Retirement for Nigel Mansell after he had fought his way up to seventh place only to have a broken bolt jam his gearbox in fifth gear. That was fairly quickly fixed in his pit but he then spun out of contention on the same lap that he rejoined the race. But fellow Englishman Derek Warwick brought his Arrows-Megatron home an excellent

Race 9 — GERMANY

Great teamwork — Senna, McLaren and Honda get it together — again.

seventh a mere seven seconds behind Boutsen's Benetton which he had chased for the whole race. Gugelmin, by taking eighth place enhanced his rapidly rising reputation and to his unalloyed delight Bernd Schneider had his first Grand Prix finish in his homeland with a well driven twelfth place behind Jonathan Palmer who had another determined drive to eleventh in a car that no-one could have got home higher.

But no-one will remember the 1988 German Grand Prix with greater regret than Philippe Alliot. Having started the race on wet tyres he made a brave decision on lap nine to change to slicks to exploit the dry line which was just beginning to emerge. As he approached the reverse leg chicane on his first lap on his 'bald' tyres Senna shot up inside him to put him off his line and on to the water-soaked asphalt where, like Piquet before, he immediately aquaplaned into the barrier and out of the race. At least he was in good company!

Prost had come to Germany outraged at comments in the French media that he was a 'coward' for having pulled out of the British Grand Prix. At Hockenheim he more than proved how misplaced those comments were. But now, in a situation where the best eleven results from the sixteen races decide the World Championship, his team-mate and only rival for the honour effectively led the series with five wins to his four. Alain had lost none of his ambition to win his third Championship though. We could expect the sparks to fly in Hungary in two weeks time!

'This short cut should save fuel!' But Michele could only finish fourth.

GERMAN GRAND PRIX

Winner: Ayrton Senna, McLaren-Honda MP4/4-05   **Fastest Lap:** Alessandro Nannini, 123.567 mph

GRID POSITION

No.	Driver
12	Senna
11	Prost
28	Berger
27	Alboreto
1	Piquet
19	Nannini
16	Capelli
2	Nakajima
20	Boutsen
15	Gugelmin
5	Mansell
17	Warwick
6	Patrese
22	De Cesaris
18	Cheever
14	Streiff
25	Arnoux
21	Larini
36	Caffi
30	Alliot
29	Dalmas
10	Schneider
9	Ghinzani
3	Palmer
33	Modena
32	Larrauri

RESULTS

Pos.	Driver	Car
1	Senna	McLaren-Honda MP4/4-05
2	Prost	McLaren-Honda MP4/4-04
3	Berger	Ferrari F187/88C-104
4	Alboreto	Ferrari F187/88C-103
5	Capelli	March-Judd 881/3
6	Boutsen	Benetton-Ford B188-05
7	Warwick	Arrows-Megatron A10B/03
8	Gugelmin	March-Judd 881/2
9	Nakajima	Lotus-Honda 100T/1
10	Cheever	Arrows-Megatron A10B/01
11	Palmer	Tyrrell-Cosworth DG/017-1
12	Schneider	Zakspeed 881/1
13	De Cesaris	Rial-Cosworth ARC1/03
14	Ghinzani	Zakspeed 881/4
15	Caffi	Dallara-Ford F188/003
16	Larrauri	EuroBrun-Cosworth 188-02
17	Arnoux	Ligier-Judd JS31/02
18	Nannini	Benetton-Ford B188-06
19	Dalmas	Lola-Cosworth LC88-03

WORLD CHAMPIONSHIP

Drivers	Pts
1. Prost	60
2. Senna	57
3. Berger	25
4. Alboreto	16
5. Piquet	15
6. Boutsen	12
7. Warwick	9
8. Nannini	6
Mansell	6
10. Palmer	5
11. Capelli	4
12. De Cesaris	3
Gugelmin	3
14. Cheever	1
Martini	1
Nakajima	1
Patrese	1

Constructors	Pts
1. McLaren-Honda	117
2. Ferrari	41
3. Benetton-Ford	18
4. Lotus-Honda	16
5. Arrows-Megatron	10
6. Williams-Judd	7
March-Judd	7
8. Tyrrell-Cosworth	5
9. Rial-Cosworth	3
10. Minardi-Cosworth	1

7th August 1988
Circuit: Hungaroring

Hungary

Q UITE simply this was the best Grand Prix of the year so far. Dramatic, interesting and exciting in practice and the same all the way through the race. Not that the result was any different from the 1988 norm — no one really expected it to be. But the making of it was in genuine doubt right up to the finish line and whether you were watching on the spot or on the box you felt that you'd seen something worth seeing.

If there was anywhere that the McLaren steam roller was going to be halted it was Hungary. As the FOCA teamsters somewhat queasily boarded the Tupolev dual-purpose airliner/bomber of the Hungarian National carrier, Malev, to fly to Budapest they were thinking of the newly created (in 1986) Hungaroring and how its characteristics would narrow the gap between the turbo and normally aspirated cars. 2.49 miles long it straddles a deep valley on the outskirts of the Capital and only has one straight of any consequence — and that not very long. The result of the gradient, the rising and falling twists and turns, the need constantly to use all the gears from second to top and the equally constant acceleration and braking is that the track is both fuel-intensive and slow by modern standards — 99 mph for the lap and only one very short opportunity to build up to a top speed of some 180 mph. So turbo lag and their fuel limitation of 150 litres was going to restrict the performance of the McLarens — the only cars likely to worry the 40 kg-lighter top 3½ litre runners with their unrestricted fuel allowance!

In practice it certainly looked like it. Friday's qualifying hour was marred by a track surface that only had a dry line in the last few minutes after torrential morning rain (surely we weren't going to have a third successive wet race?). So the first day's times were unrepresentative which meant that the grid was going to be based on the Saturday afternoon session's results. And what an exciting sixty minutes that was! For up to five minutes from the end, Nigel Mansell was in pole position in his normally aspirated Williams-Judd with a superb lap, faster even than his own 1987 pole time in a turbocharged Williams-Honda. That was achievement enough, but it was heightened by the fact that it was done by an unshaven and very jaded Nigel who was suffering from the debilitating after-effects of chicken-pox which he had caught from his Number One son Leo. We were working together at a

The nearest to pole position Riccardo has been in 1988.

Sales Conference the day before practice and had to start the day at breakfast by boring a hole in his leather belt to allow for

85

the fact that he'd lost two inches and seven pounds in four days!

It was Ayrton Senna who snatched the top grid position in the dying minutes of practice but it certainly hadn't been easy for him. The fastest lap figures at the top of the pit lane video screens changed nine times before the enthralled onlookers. First Senna. Then Prost. Prost again. And again. Mansell! Senna again. No Mansell! And finally, with a clear lap and a typically Banzai effort, Ayrton went round the Hungaroring in one minute 27.635 seconds to take his eighth pole position of 1988 and the twenty-fourth of his outstanding career. Only two drivers had now started more Grands Prix from pole — Jim Clark and Fangio. The key to Senna's achievement was that he'd typically found that vital clear lap — a very difficult thing to do at the Hungaroring. Others were saying that if they had been able to do so they felt confident that they would have been in pole position. He had. They hadn't. But behind the Brazilian there was the heartening sight of five normally-aspirated cars. Second for the second time this year, Nigel Mansell's Williams-Judd only one-tenth of a second slower than Senna.

Then, on row two, Boutsen's Benetton-Ford and Capelli's March-Judd (conclusively demonstrating both that Ivan is a very fine driver and that the ever-improving 1988 March was not just a fast-circuit car). Row three was Nannini (Benetton) and Patrese (Williams) and then — way down in seventh place after 'traffic problems' was Alain Prost's McLaren. The Ferraris? Berger ninth and Alboreto fifteenth and both thoroughly fed up with the continued inadequacies of their cars which here included 'no grip, poor response and poor handling — and tomorrow we're going to be even worse off with dreadful fuel consumption.'

In Budapest on Saturday evening with the prospects of really close competition in tomorrow's race the zithers and violins seemed especially cheerful! But it was going to be a long race. Seventy-six laps, 198.5 miles at an average speed of some 96 mph was going to take almost the maximum two hours to run and on the twisty, hard-to-pass track it was going to be a tough one too for the temperature was 27 degrees. Not a pleasant prospect for poor Nigel Mansell who'd found even an hour of intermittent practice physically exhausting.

Piquet spins. Streiff avoids. Johansson's long gone.

Race 10 — HUNGARY

From the front row of the grid Nigel made an absolutely blistering start and very nearly took the lead for the first time in 1988. But with the benefit of boost it was Senna who just got to Turn One first and who once again stayed there for the whole of the race — except for a few yards. And from the front he gave a masterly demonstration of coolness under pressure (unlike Monaco!) and of his ability to drive tactically. Every lap as he came out of the long 180 degree Turn 17 into the short straight, he was able to nourish his Honda engine with a whiff of extra boost and draw away from Mansell's nimble Williams to create a gap that made it impossible for Nigel to get close enough to outbrake the McLaren and then exploit his car's responsiveness in the wiggly bits that followed. With Senna going no faster than he had to, he was immediately followed by a five-car snake to give us the most enthralling sight we'd had all year. Tight up behind Mansell it was Riccardo Patrese who'd rocketed up from sixth to third at the first corner and right behind him were Boutsen, Nannini and Berger with Prost rapidly up to seventh from the ninth place he'd fallen to on lap one. After his fine fourth place grid position the unfortunate Capelli had blown it through over-revving on Turn One but his team-mate Mauricio Gugelmin was following Prost.

And so it excitingly continued until lap twelve when Nigel Mansell, his front wing almost under Senna's gearbox, lost downforce and spun down to fourth place behind Patrese and Boutsen. With a different Williams filling his mirrors Senna continued his policy of 'pass if you can — but first you've got to catch me on the straight' policy to stave off first Patrese and then Boutsen when a misfiring Judd engine dropped Ricardo from second to third and then sixth behind Prost, Mansell and Berger. For now Alain, having calmly picked off Berger and a faltering Nannini, who's engine was overheating, was on his way. On lap 32 he had taken Mansell and third place. Only Thierry to pass now before he could set about Senna! Five laps later into the pits came Nigel to replace the tyres which had been flat-spotted by his spin and which had been causing acute vibration. As if he hadn't got enough problems! On lap 58 he was in

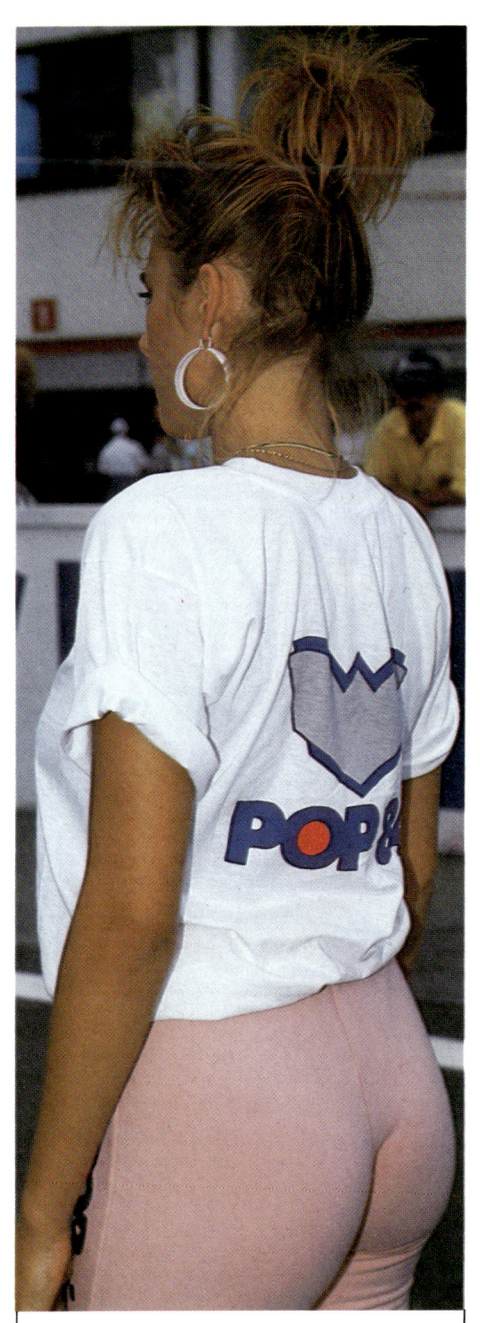

Miss Popov — a cheeky pit lane visitor.

87

TEAM ANALYSIS

LOTUS
Not a happy Hungarian GP. Revised driver-adjustable electronic dampers but cars inexplicably slow. Piquet qualifies only 13th in preferred spare car. Hits Martini's Minardi on lap nine and pits for new tyres and nosecone. Loses two laps. Finishes eighth, three laps down with clutch problem. Down a place to sixth in Championship. At disliked circuit Nakajima starts nineteenth but races reliably to seventh (three laps down).

TYRRELL
For the team's 250th Grand Prix start ex-Ferrari Harvey Postlethwaite makes his first appearance as the new Tyrrell Designer (to be joined by ex-Ferrari aerodynamicist Jean-Claude Migeot). Jonathan Palmer qualifies 21st. Retires lap four when engine cuts out. Julian Bailey impresses at first Hungaroring appearance with third fastest time in wet Friday free-practice. Switches to Palmer car when transmission breaks during Saturday timed session but fails to qualify.

WILLIAMS
A morale-boosting meeting for Team Williams at circuit NA car suits well. Despite lack of stamina caused by chickenpox, Nigel Mansell qualifies superb second only one-tenth second off pole. Ceaselessly pressures leader Senna for twelve laps until close proximity causes loss of downforce and resultant spin. Drops to fourth. To pit, lap 30, to replace flat-spotted tyres. Again, lap 59, for second set. Retires from sixth place, lap 61, completely exhausted after a magnificent effort. Amidst general belief that he is to be displaced by (Alboreto?) next year, Riccardo Patrese equally impressive. Qualifies sixth. Up to third at first corner. Runs second for eighteen laps after Mansell retirement. Drops back due to misfire. Finishes sixth for second point of year.

ZAKSPEED
Much needed Gustav Brunner (ex-Ferrari, ex-RIAL) now designing 1989 Zakspeed at Niederzissen. Existing car unable to get job done at Hungaroring. Ghinzani, involved in two car-damaging incidents on Friday, fails to qualify — as does Schneider on first visit to circuit.

McLAREN
Tenth successive win and seventh one/two finish of 1988 for McLaren but not so easy this time. With internal ducting as at Hockenheim and ceramic impellers to minimise turbo lag Senna just takes eighth pole of season one-tenth second faster than Mansell. Prost starts only seventh. Under constant pressure from Mansell, Patrese, Boutsen and Prost Senna 'races easy', conserving tyres and fuel, to superb victory and takes joint leadership of Championship with Prost. After yet another poor start Prost fights up to second place on lap 47. Momentarily takes lead, lap 49, but after making fastest lap (lap 51: one minute 30.639 seconds = 99.064 mph) drops back with left front wheel vibration problem (loose bearing). Ignores this to charge up to Senna in closing laps and finish only ½ second behind team-mate. McLaren now virtually unbeatable in Constructors' Championship and, with six wins to Prost's four Senna becomes favourite for Drivers' award.

AGS
Two completely rebuilt cars for Streiff who qualifies 23rd after balance, brake and engine problems. In nineteenth place hits Nakajima, lap eight, and pits for new nosecone. Rejoins 23rd but retires same lap when suspension breaks and jettisons wheel.

McLaren's dynamic duo. Senna leads Prost to the flag.

Race 10 — HUNGARY

After problems in practice, the colourful Tarquini/Coloni partnership finished 13th.

MARCH
Best race yet for this most impressive team. New 'Biplane' front wing helps provide razor-sharp handling. Capelli achieves highest-ever grid position at excellent fourth. Up to third at first corner but over-revs and pits for new ECU. Then retires, lap six, with massive misfire. Gugelmin starts eighth and then races against Nannini, Berger and Patrese to finish fifth with no clutch — his second points finish in three races in 'the hardest race of my life'. With third successive points finish Team very happy to have shown that their car is not only good on quick circuits.

ARROWS
A disappointing meeting. Warwick and Cheever qualify twelfth and fourteenth after engine, boost, handling, electrical, fuel injection and traffic problems. Warwick improves to seventh by lap 60 and Cheever to ninth, lap 41. Both retire with unprecedented complete loss of brakes. Cheever on lap 56 and Warwick ten laps later.

BENETTON
Boutsen again the best of the 'non McLarens'. Qualifies third only three-tenths seconds off Senna pole time and races to excellent third place (his third of 1988) and best NA driver despite being slowed by cracked exhaust pipe after running challenging second to Senna for seventeen laps. Nannini starts fifth and goes into dirt at first corner avoiding charging Patrese. Drops to seventh with overheating engine which causes lap 25 retirement.

OSELLA
Larini 21st in wet Friday Free practice but fails to pre-qualify which he is now required to do as a result of De Cesaris having scored points.

RIAL
Designer Gustav Brunner now departed to Zakspeed. Electrical problems with both cars on Friday necessitate De Cesaris qualifying on Saturday which he does — 18th. Drives strong race with sixth fastest NA lap to climb to ninth by lap 25. Retires lap 29 with broken CV joint as a result of clouting kerb during morning warm-up.

MINARDI
Testing after Hockenheim failure to qualify both cars produces revised front suspension for Sala car. Luis qualifies best yet at eleventh for first Hungaroring race. Hits Dalmas on lap one and pits for new front wheel and wing. Then drives excellent race to third eleventh place of the year. Martini, with old suspension, starts sixteenth but retires from twelfth, lap nine, after being assaulted from rear by Piquet's Lotus.

LIGIER
Frank Dernie Designer appointment unofficially confirmed for 1989. All three cars fitted with 'Swan Neck' air box. With revised front suspension Rene Arnoux qualifies 25th and much-relieved Johansson gets in at 24th. Both retire from race. Johansson, lap 20, from sixteenth place when throttle sticks open. Arnoux also from sixteenth, lap 33, with overheated engine.

FERRARI
Both cars a disaster at Hungaroring. 'No grip. No balance. No engine response.' Resigned Berger qualifies ninth and races to meritorious fourth with now customary need to conserve fuel. Thoroughly disgruntled Alboreto starts lowly fifteenth and retires, lap 41, when engine cuts out after having progressed to eighth place. With a three week gap to Belgian GP much needed improvement can hopefully be effected.

LOLA
Yet another crash affects team when Dalmas has violent shunt with Larrauri on Saturday morning. Bravely qualifies in spare car with revised rear suspension. Restores morale with excellent ninth place (three laps down) after long battle with team-mate Alliot, Tarquini and Modena. After starting twentieth Alliot finishes twelfth (four laps down) between Modena and Tarquini.

COLONI
Tarquini starts race for first time since Montreal — in 22nd place. Despite major handling problems due to rear suspension failure achieves hard fought third GP finish in thirteenth place (five laps down).

EUROBRUN
Larrauri enhances 'mobile chicane' reputation by violently coming together with Dalmas on Saturday morning. Then, to general relief, fails to qualify. Modena just gets in at 26th after myriad of problems. Races to finish eleventh despite tyre problems and misfiring engine.

DALLARA
Alex Caffi, delighted with his car's handling, qualifies in best-yet tenth place (ahead of both Lotuses, both Arrows and Alboreto). Up to ninth on lap two and stays there until lap 22 when engine goes off and forces retirement. A performance which confirms that Alex is a man to watch.

89

100% action. Philippe Alliot gives his sponsors value.

for a second set and just two laps after that he sadly drew in to his pit to retire — absolutely spent. Nigel Mansell has nothing to prove in racing but once again he had shown that when the machinery is right no one can charge harder, show more courage or drive faster.

While all this had been going on we again had the sad sight of World Champion Nelson Piquet failing to make his mark — this time at a circuit where he had won commandingly the year before. From a lowly thirteenth on the grid his Lotus-Honda had a contentious coming-together with Pierluigi Martini's Minardi which necessitated a pit visit from which he never really recovered. Eighth place, three laps down. How times change!

But up front it was starting to look the same — on lap 47, Prost was past Boutsen and in second place behind Senna — and gaining! Two laps later as Ayrton went to lap the Lola of Yannick Dalmas and the Coloni of Gabriele Tarquini at Turn One, Prost took all three of them in a breath-taking manoeuvre. But in doing so he exited the corner off-line and too fast. In less time than it takes to say

it, Senna had retaken the lead. But it was great while it lasted! Back to the attack went Alain with a fastest lap of the race on lap 51 (one minute 30.639 seconds = 99.064 mph — half a second off Piquet's 1987 Williams-Honda lap record) only to drop back some six seconds with an acute vibration caused by a loose left front wheel bearing. Boutsen closed on the Frenchman's McLaren but then, with but six laps to go Alain, realising that if Ayrton won, the first-places score would be six to four, gritted his teeth and went for it. Ignoring the vibration he inched his way up to Senna but his was a lost cause. Half a second separated the two McLarens after the full 76 laps but it was enough to even the number of points shared by 1988's two top men.

For the third time in ten races Thierry Boutsen was third to heighten his reputation with an immaculate drive marred only by the fact that, with fifteen laps to go, a broken exhaust pipe ended any chance he might have had of benefiting from a McLaren problem. Which, of course, didn't happen anyway! Fourth went to the frustrated,

Race 10 — HUNGARY

fuel-deficient Ferrari of Gerhard Berger — the last one to go the full distance, ahead of another fine drive by Mauricio Gugelmin, who took points for the second time in three races, and a sixth-placed Riccardo Patrese gloomily contemplating the possibility of losing his Williams drive in 1989.

Hungary may have produced the same result in the end but it was certainly the most entertaining Grand Prix we'd had so far. But not for Alain Prost. Without rancour and with his usual complete honesty he said 'I should have won that one. My car was faster than Ayrton's.' Senna agreed but then, as many remarked, 'he would wouldn't he!' And now, with a two-win deficit to Senna, Prost's chances of winning his third World Championship seemed to depend on Ayrton breaking down in one of the six races that were left. And a McLaren had yet to do that in 1988!

'Why should I smile — I'm lost.'

'Why should I smile — I've got to get in and drive it soon!'

'Yes I know — but it saves time when I get up!'

MURRAY WALKER'S GRAND PRIX YEAR

Ghinzani making a right ghoulash out of it — the result? Mass apathy.

HUNGARIAN GRAND PRIX

Winner: Ayrton Senna, McLaren-Honda MP4/4-05   **Fastest Lap:** Alain Prost, 99.064 mph

GRID POSITION		RESULTS			WORLD CHAMPIONSHIP			
No.	Driver	Pos. Driver	Car	Drivers	Pts	Constructors	Pts
	12 Senna	1 Senna	McLaren-Honda MP4/4-05	1. Senna	66	1. McLaren-Honda	132
5	Mansell	2 Prost	McLaren-Honda MP4/4-04	Prost	66	2. Ferrari	44
	20 Boutsen	3 Boutsen	Benetton-Ford B188-05	3. Berger	28	3. Benetton-Ford	22
16	Capelli	4 Berger	Ferrari F187/88C-104	4. Boutsen	16	4. Lotus-Honda	16
	19 Nannini	5 Gugelmin	March-Judd 881/2	Alboreto	16	5. Arrows-Megatron	10
6	Patrese	6 Patrese	Williams-Judd FW12/3	6. Piquet	15	6. March-Judd	9
	11 Prost	7 Nakajima	Lotus-Honda 100T/1	7. Warwick	9	7. Williams-Judd	8
15	Gugelmin	8 Piquet	Lotus-Honda 100T/3	8. Nannini	6	8. Tyrrell-Cosworth	5
	28 Berger	9 Dalmas	Lola-Cosworth LC88-03	Mansell	6	9. Rial-Cosworth	3
36	Caffi	10 Sala	Minardi-Cosworth M188-04	10. Gugelmin	5	10. Minardi-Cosworth	1
	24 Sala	11 Modena	EuroBrun-Cosworth 188-03	Palmer	5		
17	Warwick	12 Alliot	Lola-Cosworth LC88-04	12. Capelli	4		
	1 Piquet	13 Tarquini	Coloni-Cosworth 188-CF02	13. De Cesaris	3		
18	Cheever			14. Patrese	2		
	27 Alboreto			15. Cheever	1		
23	Martini			Martini	1		
	29 Dalmas			Nakajima	1		
22	De Cesaris						
	2 Nakajima						
30	Alliot						
	3 Palmer						
31	Tarquini						
	14 Streiff						
26	Johansson						
	25 Arnoux						
33	Modena						

92

28th August 1988
Circuit: Spa-Francorchamps

Belgium

'**DO** McLaren use the same circuit as everyone else?' one of the Team Managers plaintively asked me. For such was the superiority of the Woking Team's driver/car/engine package that only one man seemed likely to offer any opposition to Ayrton Senna and Alain Prost after qualifying for the Belgian Grand Prix on the superb Spa-Francorchamps circuit — Gerhard Berger in his Ferrari.

We had seen the McLarens win everywhere from the slow twists and turns of Monaco to the flat out sweeps of Silverstone and there didn't seem to be any reason why things should change in Belgium. Spa is one of only four places where a Grand Prix is run on public roads (Monaco, Detroit and Australia are the others) and it is regarded as the finest circuit in the world by most people. At 4.3 miles long it is situated amidst thick forests at an altitude of some 2,000 feet in the glorious hilly Ardennes countryside. It has every kind of bend and corner from the tight first gear, fifty miles an hour, hairpin at La Source to the daunting 180 mph sixth gear curve at Blanchimont. It encompasses the super-spectacular down/up, left/right full speed double bend at Eau Rouge, the long flat out drag up to Kemmel and the plunge down into the valley after the right/left bends at Les Combes. In short it is a driver's circuit and one where power and fuel efficiency are at a premium. And that is a combination where Honda reign supreme thanks to their experience, competence, thoroughness and willingness to spend what it takes.

So what was new at Spa? Martin Brundle was. On the Wednesday evening before the race a startled and not best pleased Frank Williams received a telephone call from Nigel Mansell to tell him that he had got a secondary virus infection from his post-Germany chicken-pox and that he would be unable to drive in Belgium. Which accounted for an equally startled but very pleased Brundle having the phone ring in his Jaguar Sovereign whilst he was driving home on the M11! At the end of his disastrous 1987 with Zakspeed, Martin had deliberately opted out of Formula One to drive for Jaguar in sports car races — with great success. He had resolved never to accept a Grand Prix drive again unless it was in a competitive car and this was it. Martin was back and never was anyone more welcome. His cheerful, friendly and helpful personality had been missed by all those privileged to be associated with him and everyone wished him well at Spa.

To nobody's great surprise Senna and Prost again occupied the front row of the starting grid — for the seventh time in eleven races. And that was bad news for

The Grand Prix world was delighted to welcome Martin Brundle back.

93

Alain Prost. With four victories to Senna's six he had to win in Belgium to keep his Championship hopes alive, and starting behind the hard charging Senna was not exactly a bonus. Especially as one of the few minus points about Spa is the first corner of the lap — La Source. The tight right hairpin just a couple of hundred yards from the grid is notorious for causing car-destroying collisions after the start and obviously the higher up the grid you are the less likely you are to become involved in one.

But it was Alain who got there first. Senna, usually so good when the lights turn to green, had a touch of wheelspin and this time it was Prost who shot into the led — until the uphill drag to Kemmel which was where he lost both the race and, it seemed, the 1988 World Championship. Senna had opted for a different aerodynamic set-up to Alain and it proved to be the better. At Les Combes, roughly half way round the lap, Ayrton pulled out of Prost's slipstream, outbraked him thanks to his greater downforce, passed his team-mate and just drove away to win his seventh race of the year and give himself a Championship lead which Prost would surely find impossible to overcome.

On the grid it had been the two Ferraris of Berger and Alboreto behind the McLarens and from the outset Gerhard was right up with Prost — even trying to get past to second on the first lap. But to no avail for on lap three he was into the pits with electrical problems. After a long delay he was back in the fray to put up the fastest lap of the race (2m 00.772s = 128.542 mph) before retiring on his twelfth lap to let Michele Alboreto into third place. But whilst it was now settled at the front, there was plenty going on behind the leaders. With Thierry Boutsen (sixth on the grid) occupying an energetic fourth place and trying to get to grips with Alboreto there was a three car struggle for fifth between Alessandro Nannini, Satoru Nakajima and Nelson Piquet with the Benetton sandwiched between Naka and Nelson. Nakajima ahead of Piquet? Yes indeed and showing every sign of staying there for the

Saturday practice was wet. Martin was fastest. Champion!

Race 11 — BELGIUM

Japanese driver who likes fast circuits and loathes slow ones was in his element at Spa. He had qualified eighth a place ahead of his team leader and after passing Patrese and Nannini was happily holding an impressive fifth place. Behind Piquet it was the turbocharged Arrows-Megatrons of Cheever and Warwick having yet another of their monumental battles just ahead of Patrese, Brundle, Capelli and Gugelmin.

With the first two places a foregone conclusion barring mechanical problems, which of course no one expected the meticulously prepared McLaren-Hondas to have, the interest in the race was who would finish where behind them. At half distance in the 43 lap contest Nakajima's excellent drive was over. From sixth place (passed by Piquet on lap 17) he drew into his pit for investigation of an acute misfire and when the Honda mechanics were unable to remove a jammed plug that was it. So now it was Nannini, driving like a man possessed, in sixth place followed by the Arrows duo with Derek Warwick now ahead of Cheever who was

Riccardo Patrese tells ICI's guests how to drive a Spa lap. Williams' Peter Windsor asks the questions.

immediately followed by Patrese, Capelli and Gugelmin. There was only one word for Capelli's driving — electrifying. With passing manoeuvres that had to be seen to be believed he passed first Patrese to ninth and then Cheever to eighth and Warwick to sixth. Sixth? Yes sixth because, on lap 36 with a certain third place in his grasp, a

Amazingly they all got round!

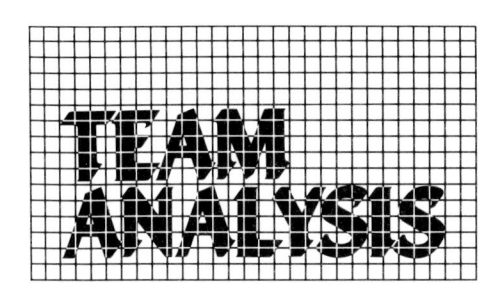

LOTUS
Another mediocre race after Team's Designer-Saviour Gerard Ducarouge announces departure at the end of the season — with Williams' defector Frank Dernie (supposedly joining Ligier) as rumoured surprise replacement. Satoru Nakajima qualifies eighth — one place higher than Piquet — prior to running excellent fifth up to lap 16. Retires from sixth place, lap 22, with misfire and jammed spark plug. After passing Nakajima, Piquet advances to fourth but, with brake bias and resultant tyre problems, drops to sixth in closing laps.

TYRRELL
No joy for Ken at Spa. For seventh time hard-trying Julian Bailey sadly fails to qualify the unimpressive 1988 Tyrrell. Jonathan Palmer starts 21st. Retires, lap 40, with broken throttle cable but is classified 14th (four laps down).

Jonathan Palmer tight in at La Source — where the famous café used to be.

WILLIAMS
After Nigel Mansell announces non-availability due to secondary virus infection following recent chicken-pox, Martin Brundle appears as very welcome returnee to Formula One. Delighted with car, he amazingly makes fastest time in wet Saturday qualifying session but starts twelfth with faster Friday time in spite of incorrect shock absorbers. Drives outstanding race to finish ninth delayed by tyre wear problem. Patrese equally impressive in his 171st GP (only Graham Hill and Jacques Laffite have started more). Qualifies superb fifth and top NA car. Drops to tenth, lap four, with tyre problem before retiring with duff engine, lap 31.

ZAKSPEED
Gustav Brunner makes first circuit appearance as Zakspeed Designer amidst rumours that team to use Yamaha engine in 1989. Thoroughly disgruntled Ghinzani qualifies 24th and retires with blown engine, lap 25, when 19th. Schneider starts his fourth GP from 25th on grid. After troubled drive at back of field with gearbox problems is classified 15th (five laps down).

McLAREN
With continued total dominance McLaren achieve their eleventh victory, eleventh pole position, seventh grid front row and eighth first and second places of 1988 to win the Constructors' Championship with a record 147 points — with five races still to go! From his ninth pole position of the season (and 25th of his career — only Jim Clark and Fangio have more) Ayrton Senna takes the lead on the first lap and holds it unchallenged to the end to win by over half a minute — his seventh 1988 win (to equal Jim Clark/Alain Prost record) and fourth successive victory. Alain Prost starts and finishes second and sportingly concedes 1988 World Championship to Senna 'who thoroughly deserves it and who I know will be a credit to the title.'

AGS
Designer Christian Vanderpleyn to leave AGS to join Coloni at season's end. Philippe Streiff starts 18th and steadily improves in race to finish twelfth (one lap down).

MARCH
Yet another excellent race for Robin Herd's most impressive team. Gugelmin and Capelli both caught out by wet Saturday final qualifying session to qualify 13th and 14th but both make superb recovery in race. Inspired Capelli finishes fifth after forceful drive which includes breathtaking passing of Patrese, Cheever, Warwick and Piquet. Gugelmin also impressive but, delayed by clutch problem and resultant spin, retires on lap 30 after having improved to eleventh.

ARROWS
Derek Warwick, 34 on Saturday, qualifies tenth with heavy flu symptoms. Depressed by 'motor which won't pick up' nevertheless grittily races full distance to finish excellent seventh only eight-tenths of a second behind Piquet. As usual Cheever starts and finishes just behind Warwick — from eleventh on the grid to eighth in the race (one lap down).

BENETTON
Best '88 race yet for Benetton in their 100th GP start (which is also the 300th GP for a Ford engine). Boutsen and Nannini (who has re-signed for 1989 and '90) start sixth and seventh. In trouble-free run in his home GP Boutsen finishes excellent third (and top NA) for the fourth time to move four points closer to Berger's third place in the Championship. Nannini races Nakajima and Piquet for 22 laps. Improves to sixth when Nakajima retires and then daringly takes fourth from Piquet for three points and Championship improvement to seventh place. Benetton now seven points closer to Ferrari's second place in Constructors' Championship.

Race 11 — BELGIUM

600 horsepower. No grip. But De Cesaris qualified an excellent ninth.

OSELLA
Larini just qualifies at 26th. Retires from 21st place on lap 13 with defective fuel pump.

RIAL
De Cesaris starts 19th after troubled Friday practice (and very encouraging ninth in Saturday's wet session). Furiously retires from eighteenth place on lap three after being rammed by the thrusting Rene Arnoux.

MINARDI
As in Germany both Martini and Sala fail to qualify.

LIGIER
Michel Tetu, Designer of the controversial and unsuccessful twin-tank Ligier to leave at end of season. Team clearly agitated over rumour that he will not now be replaced by Frank Dernie from Williams. All three cars lightened since Hungary and fitted with high-compression Judd engines. Both drivers qualify — Arnoux 17th and Johansson 20th. Arnoux grounds his car on gravel trap and retires after ramming De Cesaris when 19th on lap two. Stefan retires lap 39 (engine) but classified thirteenth.

FERRARI
In the first ever World Championship Grand Prix without the towering background presence of the great Enzo Ferrari, the Maranello team again sadly fail to score a point. Berger qualifies a promising third eight-tenths of a second off Senna's pole time with Alboreto alongside him on the second row of the grid. Gerhard a close third to the McLarens for two laps but then into the pits for a new electronic control unit. Rejoins last and makes fastest lap of race (lap ten: 128.542 mph) but retires, lap 12. Alboreto then moves to third which he retains until angrily retiring, lap 36, with blown engine. Ferrari and Berger still second and third in their respective Championships but by reduced margins.

LOLA
With minor development changes to the cars, Alliot and Dalmas qualify 16th and 23rd. Alliot has steady race to finish 11th (one lap down). Dalmas blows engine on lap ten when 22nd and retires.

COLONI
After past frustrating failures to qualify Gabriele Tarquini starts 22nd at Spa. Is disappointingly the first non-classified finisher at sixteenth (seven laps down) after being slowed by steering rack problems from lap twelve.

EUROBRUN
Larrauri fails to pre-qualify on Friday morning. Modena 29th fastest on Friday but, after failing to improve the necessary three places in Saturday's wet session, does not start the race.

DALLARA
Another quietly impressive race from both Alex Caffi and the team. Fifteenth on the grid and tenth in the race (one lap down) after chasing Martin Brundle for virtually the whole race.

97

Quiet, stylish. Brilliant. Boutsen finished third again.

furious Michele Alboreto retired with a blown engine. Poor Michele! And poor Ferrari. Both cars out in the Team's first Grand Prix since the death of the great Enzo Ferrari.

So the lonely Thierry Boutsen moved up to third in his home Grand Prix — and that was as much as he could have realistically hoped for. 'In fact it was like winning,' he said delightedly afterwards. 'There was no way I was going to beat the McLarens and I'm really pleased with the result especially as I was again the first 3½ litre driver home.' And then Piquet fourth? No way! Capelli may have been impressive but no more so than Alessandro Nannini who had made meteoric progress to close with Nelson's Lotus-Honda. Unknown to everyone except himself, Piquet had been troubled by a brake bias problem for some time. As he tried to get their balance right with the cockpit control, he was wearing his tyres which caused him to go on to the verge and collect grass in his sidepods which, in turn, made his engine overheat. And that was all Nannini needed. On lap 38, with five to go, he took Piquet at La Source with a passing move every bit as spectacular and daring as those of Capelli earlier on. But that wasn't the end of Nelson's downwards progress. Four laps later Ivan Capelli was at it again — past the Lotus into a magnificent fifth place after starting fourteenth!

So ended the Belgian Grand Prix. Throughout practice the fickle and notoriously unpredictable Ardennes weather had

Nakajima felt good after practice — he'd out-qualified Piquet!

Race 11 — BELGIUM

All Judd-powered. But Capelli passed both Gugelmin and Brundle to finish a superb fifth.

been at its variable worst. Part wet and part dry on Friday. Soaking wet on Saturday afternoon which meant that Friday's times decided the grid (although Martin Brundle, sensationally fastest on Saturday did his ambitions for a permanent return to the Grand Prix scene no harm at all). But, mercifully, it was dry all through the race. A race which, as ever, had its highs and lows. A massive high for Ayrton Senna who, with his seventh win of the season, not only virtually guaranteed himself the World Championship which he so fiercely wanted but also equalled the record shared by Jim Clark and Alain Prost. An equally massive high for McLaren whose eighth first and second places of the year made them unbeatable in the Constructors' World Championship and exceeded their own previous points record — with five races still to go! A high for the deserving normally-aspirated Benetton team with both their drivers in the first four. Highs too for both Capelli and Brundle who, in their different ways, had shown that they were very much men of the future. And for the likeable Thierry Boutsen who, with his fourth third place behind the all-conquering McLarens, had moved to within striking distance of Gerhard Berger's third place in the Championship.

But lows too. For Gentleman Racer Alain Prost who pragmatically conceeded the World Championship to Senna after the race — 'I know it is mathematically possible for me to beat Ayrton but realistically it is not. He is driving better than me at the moment. He deserves the success and he will make a very worthy Champion.' Few people other than Alain would be as truthful and generous as that. A low for Ferrari who failed to score a point for the fourth time in eleven races. And for Alboreto who must have been longing for the season to end and for a new career with another team to begin in 1989.

But that's motor racing. Some you win and some you lose. It just seemed to all the teams except one that McLaren were getting more than their fair share of the spoils! A feeling that was intensified when they heard that now that the Woking Wonders had won the Constructors' Championship and guaranteed themselves the Drivers' title too they were going for the jackpot — sixteen wins from sixteen races!

99

BELGIAN GRAND PRIX

Winner: Ayrton Senna, McLaren-Honda MP4/4-05   *Fastest Lap:* Gerhard Berger, 128.542 mph

GRID POSITION			RESULTS				WORLD CHAMPIONSHIP			
No.	Driver	Pos.	Driver	Car		Drivers	Pts		Constructors	Pts
12	Senna	1	Senna	McLaren-Honda MP4/4-05		1. Senna	75	1.	McLaren-Honda	147
11	Prost	2	Prost	McLaren-Honda MP4/4-02		2. Prost	72	2.	Ferrari	44
28	Berger	3	Boutsen	Benetton-Ford B188-02		3. Berger	28	3.	Benetton-Ford	29
27	Alboreto	4	Nannini	Benetton-Ford B188-06		4. Boutsen	20	4.	Lotus-Honda	17
6	Patrese	5	Capelli	March-Judd 881/5		5. Alboreto	16	5.	March-Judd	11
20	Boutsen	6	Piquet	Lotus-Honda 100T/2		Piquet	16	6.	Arrows-Megatron	10
19	Nannini	7	Warwick	Arrows-Megatron A10B/03		7. Warwick	9	7.	Williams-Judd	8
2	Nakajima	8	Cheever	Arrows-Megatron A10B/01		Nannini	9	8.	Tyrrell-Cosworth	5
1	Piquet	9	Brundle	Williams-Judd FW12/1		9. Mansell	6	9.	Rial-Cosworth	3
17	Warwick	10	Caffi	Dallara-Cosworth F188/003		Capelli	6	10.	Minardi-Cosworth	1
18	Cheever	11	Alliot	Lola-Cosworth LC88-04		11. Gugelmin	5			
5	Brundle	12	Streiff	AGS-Cosworth JH23/2		Palmer	5			
15	Gugelmin					13. De Cesaris	3			
16	Capelli					14. Patrese	2			
36	Caffi					15. Cheever	1			
30	Alliot					Martini	1			
25	Arnoux					Nakajima	1			
14	Streiff									
22	De Cesaris									
26	Johansson									
3	Palmer									
31	Tarquini									
29	Dalmas									
9	Ghinzani									
10	Schneider									
21	Larini									

Enzo Ferrari   Born Modena 1898. Died Modena 1988

HE came slowly into the room leaning on a stick looking frail and, as ever, wearing tinted glasses which made it difficult to see his eyes. For years it had been my ambition to be in the same room as this man — the greatest in the history of motor racing. But now I was to exceed it by interviewing him in his study at Maranello.

The world had never seen the like of Enzo Ferrari and it never will again. His long career began as a successful racing driver after which he became a brilliant Team Manager who formed and developed the legendary pre-war Scuderia Ferrari, Alfa-Romeo's Racing Division. He then went on to found his own Team and Company which became the most famous in the world. A talent spotter *par excellence*, both of drivers and engineers, he had the ability to get the best out of people — and the ruthlessness to cast them aside when they had served their purpose. Colombo, Lampredi, Jano and Forghieri designed for him. Nuvolari, Ascari, Fangio, Hawthorn, Surtees, Lauda, Villeneuve — and many other superstars — drove for him. And anyone who hadn't wished they had.

His Grand Prix cars won more races than any other. His sports cars won Le Mans, the Targa Florio and the Mille Miglia. To drive one of his road cars is the ambition of every red-blooded motorist. He was a Patriot, a cunning politician, a tough, demanding and enormously successful businessman and a gifted publicist. But above all he was an enthusiast who lived for his racing cars and as such he will always be remembered.

I am more than proud to have been in his presence.

11th September 1988
Circuit: Monza

Italy

'**SPIN! Senna! Ayrton Senna spins! And into the lead goes Berger. Into second place goes Alboreto. What a FANTASTIC situation! I am surrounded by a bunch of cheering, gesticulating, shouting, overjoyed Italians and the atmosphere is unbelievable! We are not only going to see a Ferrari win in Italy — we are going to see one finish second . . . and there is the dejected, broken-hearted Senna walking away. He has done in Italy exactly the same thing as he did in Monaco — spun out in the lead!'**

Life at Monza in the massive concrete grandstand overlooking the pits and main straight is never relaxed. No one enjoys their motor sport more than the Italians and they love to show it with plenty of noise and body language. And in all my life I've not seen anything to equal their reaction to the start of lap 50 of the 51 lap 1988 Italian Grand Prix as the above excited extract from my commentary shows!

No one could say that their enthusiasm wasn't justified. Everyone expected Round Twelve of the World Championship to be another McLaren benefit and nothing had happened in practice to make them think any differently. Ayrton Senna had taken the 26th pole position of his career and, in the process, had made it ten in one season — a record. Alain Prost was second on the grid to make it eight McLaren 'front rows' in twelve races although, very significantly as it was later to prove, he had been bothered by a persistent misfire from his Honda engine which was accompanied by a strange rear-end vibration. 'We think we've located it,' said Ron Dennis who also emphasised that there was no complacency in his organisation after eleven wins in a row and that they were all ambitious to make a clean sweep of the sixteen races. For qualifying Senna and Prost had both used the more powerful 'fast circuits' XE-3 version of the Honda V6 turbo motor although 'in the race we will be using the XE-2 engine, the settings of which are known and confirmed,' said Honda's Formula One Project Engineer (i.e., The Boss) Osamu Goto. To the great relief of Ferrari, no doubt, who were obviously desperately keen to do well on their home circuit not only to honour the memory of their great founder the recently deceased Enzo Ferrari, but also to please their new masters at Fiat.

Berger and Alboreto made up the second row of the starting grid and then, to continue the symmetry we'd become used to, it was the Arrows cars of Eddie Cheever and Derek Warwick — both absolutely delighted that Swiss engineer Heini Mader, who is responsible for their Megatron engines, had at last managed to liberate their full 2.5 bar boost by using larger Garrett turbocharger

Good friends. Race winner Gerhard Berger with his ex-Benetton boss Peter Collins.

101

The Arrows were fastest in a straight line — cornering seemed more of a problem for Derek.

casings. Nelson Piquet was next, in seventh place, to break things up a bit, but he was followed by the two Benettons of Boutsen and Nannini with Thierry's the fastest 3½ litre car in eighth place nearly three seconds slower than Senna.

No great surprises so far then but there were two, lower down the starting order — twenty-second on the grid in the number five Williams was Frenchman Jean-Louis Schlesser deputising for a still-sick Nigel Mansell, whilst in the final space was a very relieved Julian Bailey who had managed to qualify this time although, sadly, his team-mate Jonathan Palmer had not. Why no Martin Brundle in the Mansell Williams as in Belgium? Because, understandably, Jaguar were anxious that he should not jeopardise his chances of winning the World Sports Car Championship in which he held second place. And of which Jean-Louis Schlesser was the leader!

Monza, with its 3.6 mile lap record of 1m 26.796s (149.5 mph: Senna: Lotus-Honda, 1987) is very much a power circuit which

Michele Alboreto, second in his last Italian GP for Ferrari, almost caught Berger.

accounted for the fact that there were turbo cars in the first seven places on the grid. After poor Alessandro Nannini had been pushed into the pit lane for a faulty throttle position sensor to be replaced, and a big panic over getting Berger into the spare Ferrari had been resolved (sticking throttle with the race car) the two McLarens led the rest away at the start. Prost first. Then Senna. But only for a few yards for as soon as Alain

Race 12 — ITALY

Far from the madding crowd!

TEAM ANALYSIS

LOTUS
Team Lotus announce that, for 1989, Judd engine to replace Honda, Piquet to continue as No. 1 driver, Camel renewing sponsorship and Designer Gerard Ducarouge leaving to join Larrousse-Lola team. This followed by disappointing Monza. Four-times winner Nelson Piquet qualifies only seventh before sliding off track into retirement with inoperative clutch and jammed gearbox, lap 12, when eighth. Down to sixth in Championship. Nakajima starts twelfth and retires (Honda engine problem for the second successive race. Unheard of!), lap 12, when 13th.

TYRRELL
This time Bailey just qualifies and Palmer does not. Julian starts 26th and drives trouble-free race at rear of field to finish twelfth (two laps down). A well-deserved confidence booster.

WILLIAMS
Nigel Mansell again reports sick with continued virus problems. 'Red Five' taken over by World Sports Car Championship leader Frenchman Jean-Louis Schlesser who qualifies 22nd for his first GP. Then achieves 'Tifosi' approval by inadvertently T-Boning race-leader Ayrton Senna into retirement on lap 50. Recovers to finish praiseworthy eleventh. Patrese tenth on grid. To seventh lap one and then fierce battle with Warwick and Capelli. Passed by both but finishes seventh after Prost and Senna retirements.

A memorable debut! At this very spot Jean-Louis Schlesser later rammed Ayrton Senna.

Sadness for Schneider at Monza. Up to eleventh in only his fifth Grand Prix — then out.

ZAKSPEED
Team announce use of Works Yamaha engine in 1989 — a major coup. Best grid positions of 1988 with Schneider 15th and Ghinzani 16th. Both drivers retire from race at approximately half distance with blown engines due to suspected too-lean mixture, (Ghinzani lap 26 when 17th. Schneider lap 29 when eleventh).

McLAREN
Team's long-running dominance broken at Monza. After Honda announce that they will be supporting McLaren exclusively in 1989, Senna and Prost again take top two places on the grid — for the eighth time in twelve races. From record-breaking tenth pole position in one season Senna takes lead at start followed by Prost with misfiring engine (after persistent problems in practice). Prost retires lap 35. Senna richens mixture, slows and allows gap to Berger Ferrari to narrow to only six seconds but then collides with Schlesser's Williams at start of penultimate lap. With car jammed on kerb, retires amidst destroyed McLaren dreams of whitewash season.

AGS
With the loss of its big sponsor (Bouygues) and its major design personnel the little AGS team seem to have lost their way at Monza. New narrow track and revised flat bottom for car to suit fast circuits, but Streiff qualifies only 23rd. Works way up to 12th, lap 29, but retires two laps later with transmission problem.

MARCH
Another successful Grand Prix for the Leyton House Team with its fifth successive finish in the points. After a (by their high standards) not particularly encouraging eleventh (Capelli) and thirteenth (Gugelmin) places on the grid both drivers outstanding in the race. Despite front wheel vibration after hitting Patrese on the first corner Capelli impoves six places to go the full distance and finish fifth as top NA Driver. Gugelmin slowed by down-on-power engine and no clutch from lap ten but still does full 51 laps to finish eighth.

Race 12 — ITALY

ARROWS
Certainly one of Arrows' best Grands Prix ever. With revised turbos which liberate full 2.5 bar boost Cheever and Warwick (who re-signs for 1989) take fine fifth and sixth places on grid. Cheever, fastest of all (in a straight line) in practice at 200.7 mph, improves to fourth, lap 35, with Prost retirement, and then to third, lap 50, as Senna walks home. Warwick, feeling fit after long time below par, drops to tenth lap one but then fights past Capelli, Patrese, and Boutsen to finish fourth only six-tenths of a second behind Cheever. With first podium finisher since Italy 1983 and both drivers in top four Arrows jump two places to equal-fourth in Constructors' Championship.

BENETTON
Once again Benetton the class of the NA field in practice with Boutsen starting eighth and Nannini ninth behind seven turbos. Nannini starts from the pit lane, a lap down, after a throttle position sensor fails on the grid. Then drives a stunning race to finish ninth, one lap down, with the fifth fastest lap of all (slower only than those of Alboreto, Berger, Senna and Prost). Boutsen qualifies eighth (fastest N/A) and goes full distance to finish sixth with down-on-power engine — his seventh points score from twelve 1988 races.

OSELLA
Nicola Larini qualifies 17th but retires lap three (electrics) when 20th.

RIAL
After starting from 18th on the grid Andrea De Cesaris improves to twelfth by lap 15. Then, in battle with Schneider and Caffi, hits kerb, damages steering rack and undertray and has to retire on lap 28.

MINARDI
Designer Caliri elbowed and completely new front suspension fitted (big improvement). After recent failures to qualify both cars great Team relief when Martini and Sala make the Monza grid — 14th and 19th. Martini then retires from 15th on lap 16 with engine problem and broken undertray after kerb-hopping. Sala spins from 17th to 24th, lap five, and stays there until retiring, lap 13, with gearbox failure.

LIGIER
With no designer (Tetu gone and Dernie allegedly not joining) morale low at Ligier. Nevertheless Arnoux attempts to evaluate new side pod and radiator configuration but fails to do so due to inability to get enough laps in before something goes wrong. Qualifies 24th in 'old' car which he then nurses to 13th and last (two laps down) despite failing oil pressure and rooted tyres 'because Guy asked me to finish.' For the fifth time Johansson fails to qualify.

FERRARI
If they'd scripted it, it couldn't have been better! First and second plus fastest lap at the first Italian Grand Prix since the death of Enzo Ferrari. Gerhard Berger third in practice 0.7 secs slower than Senna with Alboreto fourth. Then a formation Berger/Alboreto drive behind the McLarens until Prost retires lap 35 and Senna pushed off lap 50. Amidst scenes of unforgettable crowd-euphoria Berger just beats hard-charging Alboreto (race fastest lap = 1m 29.070s = 145.625 mph) trying to win his last Italian GP in a Ferrari after early gearbox problem. Fifteen resultant Championship points reinforce Ferrari second place in Constructors' Championship.

LOLA
Team announce that designer Gerard Ducarouge to join them from Lotus for 1989. Alliot and Dalmas qualify 20th and 25th. Both fail to finish. Alliot out with engine problem on lap 25 when 17th out of 20. Dalmas retires (gearbox) lap 18 when 20th out of 21.

COLONI
With major aerodynamic and bodywork changes to the 188 the cheerful Gabriele Tarquini gets through pre-qualifying but only has 29th fastest time after Saturday. So no drive on Sunday.

EUROBRUN
Larrauri fails to pre-qualify on Friday morning. Modena 30th and slowest after Saturday afternoon session so does not make 'Top 26' for race. He richly deserves a better car.

DALLARA
Alex Caffi 21st on grid. To 18th lap one. Thirteenth by lap 15 and racing De Cesaris and Schneider. Retires from 13th lap 25 (electrics).

Thierry's tenth 1988 finish — and his seventh in the points.

engaged third gear the Honda misfire returned. And that was all that Senna needed. Up to the front he went and at the end of the first lap it was Senna two seconds ahead of Prost who was immediately followed by Berger and then Alboreto, Cheever, Boutsen, Patrese, Piquet, Capelli and Warwick.

For 29 laps there was no change to the first six. Prost, knowing that he had to win this one if his slim mathematical chance of regaining the Championship was to be kept alive, did his considerable best to catch Senna, but, hampered by his engine problem, never got closer than just under three seconds. It may have been interestingly static at the front, but behind Boutsen there was a magnificent fight going on for seventh place with Derek Warwick as the star. He had dropped down to tenth on the first lap but now he was on his way! Up to ninth on lap twelve as Nelson Piquet slid off the track ('My clutch had gone and I was jammed in gear'). Then to eighth past Capelli on lap 16. To seventh past Patrese on lap 22. And then, after another head-down eight fighting laps, into sixth place and the points past Thierry Boutsen's Benetton! And while all this was going on Boutsen's team-mate Alessandro Nannini was making an equally dramatic recovery. After his pit-lane start as Senna came through to begin his second lap Nannini was showing us what might have been. On his 33rd lap he made the fifth fastest tour of the day (1m 30.248s — beaten only by the McLarens and the Ferraris) and was up to eleventh place with more to come.

It was at this stage that it became clear that Prost was in trouble. For several laps his engine sounded strangely flat and on lap 34 it gave up. Into the pits he came for a long discussion amongst the Honda men about what to do, which ended with the sight of Alain stepping out of his car for his second retirement of 1988. Senna was now in an impregnable positon some 25 seconds ahead of Berger — and 'Del Boy' was up to fifth! The pragmatic Ayrton's action was clear. Warned by the Honda people to richen his mixture in view of Prost's engine problem (and Nakajima's retirement with an unexplained Honda defect) he slowed down in the knowledge that, with sixteen laps to go, he could afford to give away well over a second a lap to Gerhard and still win easily. A win which would create another record — eight victories in one season. So as Berger's Ferrari got closer and closer no one got unduly agitated about it. But with four laps still to go Berger had the McLaren clearly in sight and was closing fast. And that was different! Gerhard said to me afterwards 'I was keeping up the pressure as much as I could. If you don't do that the guy in front can relax and avoid making mistakes but if you keep pushing anything can happen.'

And at the start of the penultimate it did! Blasting down the main straight past the pits and grandstands at almost 200 miles an hour, Senna was closing fast on Jean-Louis Schlesser's Williams as they both approached the left/right/left/right Rettifilio chicane. Realising that if he didn't get past the Frenchman he would be slowed and give Berger a chance to get even closer, Senna dived inside the Williams as Jean-Louis moved to the right to give him room. So far so good, but Schlesser's wide line took him up on the kerb where he plain lost control, recovered, and T-Boned the McLaren as he shot back on to the track. Senna half-spun and ended up on the kerb with all four wheels clear of the ground. His race was over. I suppose there will be arguments about who was to blame for years to come but to me it was just a racing accident with neither driver really at fault. In his dignified way Senna seemed to agree for he merely said, 'what's done is done. I was under no pressure and of course it was a big disappointment.' When Jean-Louis went to apologise afterwards there were no harsh words.

But the excitement wasn't over yet! In his last Italian Grand Prix for Ferrari, Michele Alboreto clearly felt he had something to prove. He had overcome a problem he had had earlier in the race with his gearbox jumping out of fourth and now he was closing on Berger. After making the fastest lap of the race (1m 29.070s = 145.625 mph) on lap 44 he was almost on Gerhard's gearbox as they raced down to the finish. The Austrian staved him off to win but only just — the gap between them as they crossed the line was half a second! Italy

Race 12 — ITALY

In the drive of the day Nannini went from last to ninth.

This time Julian Bailey qualified and Jonathan Palmer didn't.

Seventh place for Riccardo — and renewal of his Williams contract for 1989.

exploded and justifiably so but there was still more to come for Derek Warwick had done to Cheever what Alboreto had done to Berger — closed right up on the last lap. And like Michele he lost the place by just over half a second!

With Ferraris first and second, the 'Roman/American' Eddie Cheever third, Capelli fifth, Patrese seventh and Nannini a superb ninth it was a great day for Italy and the traditional course invasion by the Tifosi to cheer their heroes had to be experienced to be believed. I know because I was in the middle of it fighting my way through to interview three very happy men! Real excitement had returned to the Grand Prix scene in this great race and the McLaren winning mould had been broken — albeit with more than a modicum of luck for Ferrari. But then, as Gerhard had said, 'if you keep pushing anything can happen!'

PS: In the Parc Ferme after the race there was, to put it mildly, a tense atmosphere when it was found that Berger's petrol tank could seemingly hold more than the maximum 150 litres. In the end it turned out to be a measurement error but for a while there was talk of disqualification. I'd hate to have been the man who had to make the decision!

MURRAY WALKER'S GRAND PRIX YEAR

Pressure from the man in second place caused Senna's downfall — just as it had in Monaco.

ITALIAN GRAND PRIX

Winner: Gerhard Berger, Ferrari F187/88C-104 **Fastest Lap:** Michele Alboreto, 145.625 mph

GRID POSITION			RESULTS			WORLD CHAMPIONSHIP			
No.	Driver	Pos.	Driver	Car	Drivers	Pts	Constructors	Pts
12	Senna	1	Berger	Ferrari F187/88C-104	1. Senna	75	1. McLaren-Honda	147
	11 Prost	2	Alboreto	Ferrari F187/88C-103	2. Prost	72	2. Ferrari	59
28	Berger	3	Cheever	Arrows-Megatron A10B/01	3. Berger	37	3. Benetton-Ford	30
	27 Alboreto	4	Warwick	Arrows-Megatron A10B/03	4. Alboreto	22	4. Lotus-Honda	17
18	Cheever	5	Capelli	March-Judd 881/5	5. Boutsen	21	Arrows-Megatron	17
	17 Warwick	6	Boutsen	Benetton-Ford B188-02	6. Piquet	16	6. March-Judd	13
1	Piquet	7	Patrese	Williams-Judd FW12/3	7. Warwick	12	7. Williams-Judd	8
	20 Boutsen	8	Gugelmin	March-Judd 881/2	8. Nannini	9	8. Tyrrell-Cosworth	5
19	Nannini	9	Nannini	Benetton-Ford B188-06	9. Capelli	8	9. Rial-Cosworth	3
	6 Patrese	10	Senna	McLaren-Honda MP4/4-05	10. Mansell	6	10. Minardi-Cosworth	1
16	Capelli	11	Schlesser	Williams-Judd FW12/1	11. Cheever	5		
	2 Nakajima	12	Bailey	Tyrrell-Cosworth DG/017-2	Gugelmin	5		
15	Gugelmin	13	Arnoux	Ligier-Judd JS31/02	Palmer	5		
	23 Martini				14. De Cesaris	3		
10	Schneider				15. Patrese	2		
	9 Ghinzani				16. Martini	1		
21	Larini				Nakajima	1		
	22 De Cesaris							
24	Sala							
	30 Alliot							
36	Caffi							
	5 Schlesser							
14	Streiff							
	25 Arnoux							
29	Dalmas							
	4 Bailey							

108

25th September 1988
Circuit: Estoril

Portugal

THE Italian Grand Prix at Monza two weeks earlier had shown us that the McLarens were not, after all, invincible. Ferrari's magnificent first and second places there had put new heart into the Woking team's rivals and there was an excited air of expectancy when practice began at the impressive Estoril Autodromo. Every one of the four World Championship races which had been held there since it was first used for the Portuguese event in 1984 had been a really good one, and the hopes were that 1988 would continue the tradition.

Indeed this year might even enhance it for the Estoril circuit is very different to Monza where only Ferrari could realistically have hoped to beat McLaren. Monza is flat, very fast and calls primarily for sheer power. Estoril has two fast sections — the long 185 mph bottom straight and the 'kinked' straight (if you see what I mean!) which roughly parallels it — but it also has gradient and six second or third gear bends which demand more than sheer grunt. To do well in Portugal your car needs to have good brakes, good throttle response, sharp handling and very good fuel efficiency. Plus, if you're driving, plenty of stamina for it is hot and the surface is very bumpy indeed. So bumpy in fact that the jarring the drivers were getting was breaking up their voices when they used their car-to-pits radios.

With all this in mind the 3½ litre normally aspirated teams saw themselves in with a chance of doing better in Portugal than they'd done anywhere else so far. Ayrton Senna's best McLaren time with full tanks in Saturday morning's free practice was 1m 21.64s. 'We can do that,' said one of the March-Judd team and Sunday's final half-hour practice period — the only one which enables a fair comparison to be made of the cars in race conditions — proved him right. Mauricio Gugelmin's March-Judd time was 1m 21.70s. Boutsen's, in the Benetton-Ford, was 1m 21.43s and Alain Prost, quickest of all in his McLaren, was only ¹/₁₀s faster than Thierry. With seven 3½ litre cars in the top ten it looked as though things were going to be very interesting!

But Sunday's so-called 'Warm Up' doesn't decide the grid. The two one-hour sessions on Friday and Saturday afternoons do. And when the chequered flag went out at 1400 hours on Saturday afternoon to conclude

Sala's shunt stopped practice. The only damage was Minardi's bank balance.

two days of 30 degree, sun-drenched, practising it was Alain Prost who had earned the right to start from the front space on the staggered grid. A lot of people who should know better had written the Frenchman off after Senna's dominance over him since the British Grand Prix. But at Estoril Alain showed how wrong they were. For the first time since Silverstone he was completely happy with his car and it really showed in both his manner and his performance. With fifteen minutes of the last session to go he made his usual smooth and unspectacular way round the Autodromo in a searing 1m 17.411s — faster than Gerhard Berger's 1987 Ferrari time with four-bar boost — and then pulled into his garage, got out, changed into shirt and slacks and casually but conspicuously stood around in the pit lane. As if to say 'try that one for size Ayrton — and do better if you can!' He couldn't, so pole position was Prost's with Senna second (McLaren's ninth front row of 1988). But a sensational third was Ivan Capelli's 'atmospheric' March-Judd ahead of Berger's turbocharged Ferrari, Gugelmin's March and Mansell's Williams. Three Judd-powered 'atmos' in the top six — things were indeed different at Estoril.

And yes Mansell was back. Fit and cheerful after missing the Belgian and Italian Grands Prix due to chicken pox and its debilitating after-effects, but wryly commenting that his neck muscles were finding it hard going in Portugal.

In 1987 the very first corner of the race had seen a multiple collision involving eight cars which caused the race to be stopped. It didn't even get that far this year! As Roland Bruynseraede pressed the green light button Andrea De Cesaris stalled his engine so the black and red flags went out to stop the 70 lap race. Try again — this time for 69 laps. But the second time around Derek Warwick stalled his Megatron motor and was rammed by De Cesaris! This in turn caused Sala to hit Nakajima's Lotus, knock the right front wheel off his Minardi and necessitate the race being stopped again. So try once more 38 minutes after the original start. Refuelled for a full-distance 70 laps, 189.2 miles.

To the unalloyed joy of the pro Senna Portuguese crowd, liberally laced with seemingly thousands of happy, chanting flag waving Brazilians, Ayrton shot into the lead ahead of his team-mate. He was still there at the end of the lap followed by Prost, Capelli, Berger, Mansell, Gugelmin, Piquet, Alboreto, Patrese and Boutsen. But approaching the downhill Turn One Prost bobbed out of Senna's slipstream to shoot up the inside of Ayrton's McLaren as they lined up for the fourth gear, 145 mph right-hander. As he did so Senna blatantly moved across on him and very nearly pushed him into the solid pit lane wall — to Alain's anger. 'It was quite unnecessary. Now is not the time to talk about it but I will be doing so with him!' In turn Senna stated that he was vastly unimpressed with the way Prost had forced him towards the grass at the start. Maybe the veneer of friendship between the two McLaren men was wearing thin as their World Championship rivalry increased the pressure on them?

Alain got through though. Into a lead he was never to lose on his way to his 33rd Grand Prix victory — his third in Portugal in five years but, more importantly, his fifth of 1988 and the one he needed to preserve his hopes of another World Championship. So Senna finished second this time then? Not a bit of it! There had been some worried faces in the turbo teams before the race began because for them, fuel consumption at Estoril looked to be critical — and in Senna's case it was. With a cockpit digital fuel read-out giving him bad news he was having to go very carefully as a result of which,

Lap 2 Prost gets by — split seconds earlier Senna's McLaren seemed to be sending Alain into the pit wall.

Race 13 — PORTUGAL

Boutsen's third place was his fifth of the season.

TEAM ANALYSIS

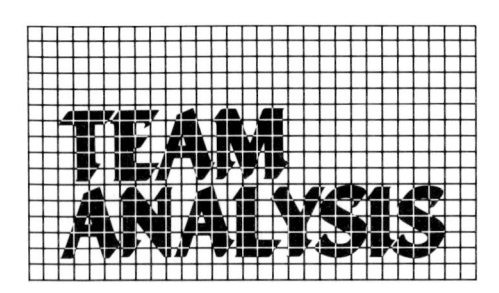

ZAKSPEED
For fifth time in thirteen races both Ghinzani and Schneider fail to qualify. 'Our chassis is just too slow and at Jerez it will be even worse!'

McLAREN
In a new chassis a very determined Alain Prost takes pole position (faster than Berger 1987 with four-bar boost) with Senna second to achieve Team's ninth 1988 grid front row. With wary eye on fuel consumption Prost then dominates race in 'perfect car' to take fifth win of season (33rd of career) and regain World Championship lead. With fuel

The only clouds in Portugal were dust — this time Patrese was responsible.

LOTUS
Second successive complete failure for Team Lotus amidst continued strongly denied rumours that ownership to change hands. Piquet drops from third to eighth on grid in final practice session. Races seventh against Alboreto, Patrese and Boutsen for 28 laps. Pits with clutch/gearbox problem lap 30 (as Monza). Rejoins but, with no improvement, retires from 17th, lap 35. Nakajima qualifies 16th after stomach-trouble following meal in Japanese restaurant! Savaged by Sala at first re-start. Damaged rear wing replaced for race but slides off track with acute oversteer to retire from 17th, lap 16.

TYRRELL
Julian Bailey sadly fails to qualify (for the eighth time) by $^{12}/_{100}$th of second. Palmer starts 22nd. Runs towards rear of field before retiring, lap 53, with severe engine-oriented vibration.

WILLIAMS
Nigel Mansell (with re-grown moustache!) re-joins team after two-race absence (chicken pox). Qualifies well at sixth despite neck strain. In fifth place closes on Senna/Capelli/Berger and then harries Senna mercilessly after Berger retirement. Retires from fourth, lap 55, after hitting Senna when lapping Jonathan Palmer and then thumping armco — hard. From eleventh on grid Patrese contests seventh with Piquet/Alboreto for 28 laps. Retires lap 29 with punctured radiator.

read-out indicating high consumption Senna slides back to sixth after precautionary eight second tyre stop on lap 56 — only to discover ample fuel in tank at race end. Team's twelfth win equals its own 1984 record with three races still to go.

AGS
After seven retirements in last eight races Philippe Streiff achieves highest-yet 1988 place with encouraging ninth (two laps down) from 21st on grid despite having to slow with worn tyres.

MARCH
Superb meeting for the cheeriest team in Grand Prix racing. Best-ever grid situation with Capelli third and Gugelmin fifth. Fully exploiting outstanding chassis and aerodynamics Capelli sensationally fights Senna for second place, takes it on lap 22 and retains it to end of race. Finishes only 9½ seconds behind Prost with third fastest lap of race (fastest NA). Gugelmin starts fifth. Passed by Mansell but holds sixth for 35 laps. Then to excellent fifth for eleven laps before lap 60 retirement with broken clutch and resultant engine problem. Team's sixth successive race in points lifts it to fifth in Constructors' Championship only one point behind Arrows.

ARROWS
Team maintains best-ever season form. From tenth on grid Derek Warwick steadily improves with typical fighting

Race 13 — PORTUGAL

drive to take fourth fourth-place of 1988 in spite of vibration problem, double vision, 'very tired left arm' and two tyres down to canvas! Multiple problems result in Cheever starting only 18th. Retires from 15th, lap ten, with broken turbocharger.

BENETTON
Nannini ninth (balance problems) and Boutsen 13th (misfire) on grid. 'We have never qualified well in Portugal.' Nannini into pits at end first lap to change wheel after clipping barrier. Then repeats stirring Monza drive including, for a time, fastest lap of race, to climb to ninth from 26th by lap 42. Into pits for tyre change and rear suspension check, lap 52, before retiring with severe vibration problems. Boutsen tenth laps 1-29 chasing Piquet/Alboreto/Patrese. Improves to fourth, lap 57, thanks to retirements but then passes fuel-starved Alboreto on last lap to go full distance and take fifth third-place of season and regain fourth position in Championship (top NA driver).

OSELLA
Larini qualifies 25th. In last place for virtually whole race but keeps going to take last classified place, tenth, five laps down.

RIAL
An eventful afternoon for Andrea De Cesaris (who will drive for Dallara in 1989). Causes first race stoppage by stalling in well-earned twelfth place on grid. In spare car then rams Warwick Arrows when Derek stalls at second start. Back in repaired race car runs twelfth for ten laps but retires, lap twelve, with broken drive-shaft.

MINARDI
Designer-less team well-pleased with Martini 14th and Sala 19th on grid. Martini retires from 13th, lap 28, with dropped engine valve. Sala collides with Nakajima at second start. Switches to spare car for third start and drives good race for best-yet finish — eighth (two laps down).

LIGIER
Both drivers qualify for only eighth time in 1988 (Arnoux 23: Johansson 24). Johansson retires from 17th, lap five, (engine). Arnoux hangs on for best finish of season so far — tenth (two laps down).

FERRARI
Despite John Barnard attendance and engine mods to improve power and fuel efficiency both drivers disappointed in practice. Berger fourth (behind Capelli's March) and Alboreto seventh (behind three NA drivers) on grid. Berger passes Senna to third, lap 23, but unable to catch Capelli although makes fastest lap of race (lap 31: 1m 21.961s = 118.652 mph). Inadvertent discharge of fire extinguisher on lap 36 'freezes' his right leg and causes retirement spin into gravel trap due to foot slipping off brake pedal. Alboreto up to fourth with retirements, lap 55. Passes Senna to third, lap 56. Coasts over line to finish fifth after being passed by Boutsen and Warwick on last lap as fuel runs out due to faulty digital read-out. Down to fifth in Championship.

A few more drops of Agip and Michele would have been on the rostrum again.

LOLA
Dalmas and Alliot start 15th and 20th. Yannick retires from 18th, lap 21, with broken alternator belt. Philippe out lap eight when 18th (engine).

COLONI
After stopping Saturday timed practice with spin into gravel trap Tarquini scrapes on to grid at 26th. Races at rear of field to finish eleventh (five laps down) after slowing from lap 50 with engine problem.

EUROBRUN
Team's appalling first GP season continues on low note with third successive failure of both drivers to qualify (Modena 29th fastest: Larrauri 31st).

DALLARA
The amply-funded, well presented Scuderia Italia again impresses. Caffi starts 17th and drives spirited race to highest-ever GP finish (seventh, one lap down) with ninth fastest lap of race (fifth fastest NA).

Better and better! Caffi came seventh — his highest finish so far.

113

whilst Prost built a seven second lead, Senna had got an inspired Ivan Capelli snapping at his gearbox.

Race by race the ever-cheerful March team had steadily been getting better and better and in Portugal they were superb. 'I honestly think Adrian Newey has given us the best chassis of them all,' said Team Manager Ian Phillips and there was clearly nothing wrong with its Judd V8 engine either! For lap after lap the ebullient Ivan Capelli (one of Grand Prix racing's nicest people) gave Senna absolutely no respite. On lap 22, to general excitement, he outbraked the Brazilian, shot past him and proceeded to open up a healthy gap. Almost as close to Capelli as Ivan had been to Senna was Gerhard Berger and a lap later the Ferrari too was past the McLaren — up into third place. Try as he may though even Berger at his best couldn't get to grips with Capelli whose flamboyant driving in his pin-sharp March was a joy to watch.

So now, with Senna an unaccustomed fourth, all eyes were on Nigel Mansell who'd passed Gugelmin to fifth on the first lap and was doggedly trying to dispose of his other long-standing Brazilian 'foe'. Recalling memories of their dramatic coming-together in Belgium 1987, which resulted in both of them spinning off, Nigel was all over Senna's McLaren. He would close right up on the corners only to lose out to Ayrton's Honda-superiority on the 'power' bits of the lap. He never did get by but on lap 36 he was up to fourth — and Senna back to third — because of an amazing incident.

As Berger lined up his third-placed Ferrari behind Capelli to take Turn One he completely lost it and spun out of contention into the deep gravel trap. 'He was worried about tyre wear before the race began,' I said. 'They've obviously gone off and that was his problem.' Wrong! (and sorry Goodyear!) He had accidentally activated his cockpit fire extinguisher whose CO_2 gas had frozen his right leg and caused his foot to slip off the brake pedal! But he had the consolation, at the end of the race, of knowing that he had made the fastest lap in his chase of Capelli (lap 31: 1m 29.961s = 118.652 mph).

Gerhard's cockpit fire extinguisher went off and so did he after the CO_2 numbed his leg.

Race 13 — PORTUGAL

'If only I could remember where I put the steering wheel!' Andrea again contemplates his early finish.

So, with poor Gerhard the victim of a freak occurrence, back to Mansell now harrying Senna for third. On lap 55 they both came upon Jonathan Palmer and in the manoeuvring to lap him Nigel clipped the rear of the McLaren, shot off the course, hit the armco hard and increased his miserable 1988 'DNF's' to ten. But while all this had been going on there was an equally intriguing situation behind the leaders.

For 29 laps, with Gugelmin's March sixth, Nelson Piquet, in seventh place, had been fighting hard to keep Alboreto, Patrese and Boutsen behind him. The pressure was eased a bit when Riccardo succumbed to a split radiator after a fine drive in ninth place but on lap 30 Nelson's fight was over with the same clutch and gearbox failures that had stopped him at Monza. No points for the World Champion for the seventh time in thirteen races.

So, on lap 55, with Berger, Mansell, and Piquet out and Gugelmin in trouble, Michele Alboreto was up to fourth. A lap later he was third — past the hapless Senna who was haltered by his low fuel reading, and on lap 57 Ayrton's misery was compounded when Boutsen and Warwick swept past him to fourth and fifth. But in this intriguing, incident-packed, race there was more to come. On the very last lap with third place in his grasp Alboreto felt his Ferrari V6 engine falter and stutter as he approached the finish line. He was running out of fuel despite a reading which indicated that he had plenty left. As he exited the last corner he suffered the agony of being passed by Boutsen's Benetton as Thierry took his fifth third-place of the season and Derek Warwick as he finished fourth for the fourth time in 1988.

A race to remember! The Portuguese Grand Prix had almost seen the first 3½ litre win of the year, for the brilliant Capelli was only 9½ seconds behind a fuel-marginal Prost when he finished. With Alboreto fifth and Senna sixth (with plenty of fuel it ironically transpired) there may have been four turbo cars in the top six but none of their drivers were looking forward to the Spanish Grand Prix on the slower and much twistier course at Jerez in a week's time. It was going to be even tougher for them there — 'in fact,' said Alain Prost 'we could be beaten.'

In its closing stages the 1988 season was proving very interesting indeed!

Mansell harries Senna — great racing until Nigel clipped Palmer's Tyrrell and went off.

115

MURRAY WALKER'S GRAND PRIX YEAR

Stefan hides his car.

Philippe hides his seat.

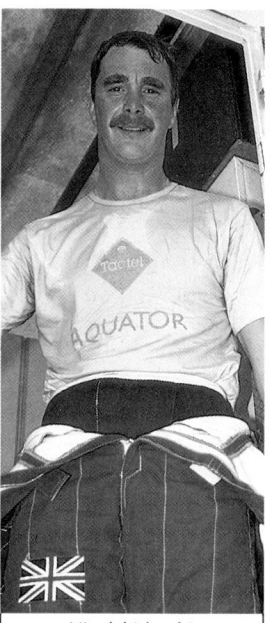

Nigel hides his disappointment.

PORTUGUESE GRAND PRIX

Winner: Alain Prost, McLaren-Honda MP4/4-06   *Fastest Lap:* Gerhard Berger, 118.652 mph

GRID POSITION		RESULTS			WORLD CHAMPIONSHIP			
No.	Driver	Pos.	Driver	Car	Drivers	Pts	Constructors	Pts
	11 Prost	1	Prost	McLaren-Honda MP4/4-06	1. Prost	81	1. McLaren-Honda	157
12	Senna	2	Capelli	March-Judd 881/5	2. Senna	76	2. Ferrari	61
	16 Capelli	3	Boutsen	Benetton-Ford B188-02	3. Berger	37	3. Benetton-Ford	34
28	Berger	4	Warwick	Arrows-Megatron A10B/03	4. Boutsen	25	4. Arrows-Megatron	20
	15 Gugelmin	5	Alboreto	Ferrari F187/88C-103	5. Alboreto	24	5. March-Judd	19
5	Mansell	6	Senna	McLaren-Honda MP4/4-05	6. Piquet	16	6. Lotus-Honda	17
	27 Alboreto	7	Caffi	Dallara-Cosworth F188/003	7. Warwick	15	7. Williams-Judd	8
1	Piquet	8	Sala	Minardi-Cosworth M188-04	8. Capelli	14	8. Tyrrell-Cosworth	5
	19 Nannini	9	Streiff	AGS-Cosworth JH23/2	9. Nannini	9	9. Rial-Cosworth	3
17	Warwick	10	Arnoux	Ligier-Judd JS31/02	10. Mansell	6	10. Minardi-Cosworth	1
	6 Patrese	11	Tarquini	Coloni-Cosworth FC188/1	11. Cheever	5		
22	De Cesaris	12	Larini	Osella-Alfa FAIL/2	Gugelmin	5		
	20 Boutsen				Palmer	5		
23	Martini				14. De Cesaris	3		
	29 Dalmas				15. Patrese	2		
2	Nakajima				16. Martini	1		
	36 Caffi				Nakajima	1		
18	Cheever							
	24 Sala							
30	Alliot							
	14 Streiff							
3	Palmer							
	25 Arnoux							
26	Johansson							
	21 Larini							
31	Tarquini							

2nd October 1988
Circuit: Jerez

Spain

IF you've been to the Portuguese Grand Prix you don't fly to the Spanish race in Jerez. You drive there. And it's a stunning journey. From Estoril to Lisbon. Over the awe-inspiring suspension bridge which soars high above the River Tagus and which, like Rio de Janeiro, is dominated by a gigantic statue of Christ. South to Setubal on the Rio Sado. To Beja. Over the border (get there before siesta time!) for, in blazing heat, a long, tiring and twisty haul through the most glorious 'Wild West' scenery to Seville. Then it's a blast down the motorway to Jerez a few miles inland from the Gulf of Cadiz. It's about 450 miles and when you arrive you know you've done them!

The Spanish Grand Prix was the last European round of the season and with only a week between races the teams went straight to Jerez from Estoril to prepare their cars for the following weekend's race. The rest of us followed on fully expecting to see an even more gripping contest than we'd just enjoyed in Portugal for if the 2.6 mile Jerez circuit had been deliberately designed to eliminate the performance gap between the turbo cars and their normally-aspirated rivals they couldn't have done a better job. It has no long straights for the turbos to wind themselves up on and it has sixteen corners, including six second or third gear changes and two hairpins. It is hard on brakes, hard on tyres and very hard on fuel consumption. Immediate throttle response is a must. And that, of course is what the turbo cars haven't got! Ally that to the fact that the normally aspirated cars have unlimited fuel and are 40kg lighter and it's understandable that the 3½ litre teams were feeling bullish.

But there's an odd atmosphere at Jerez. The Gonzalez Byass Tio Pepe sherry people have poured muchio pesetas into making the place as ideal as they can. Excellent facilities for the teams in the way of paddock and garages. Enormous grandstands and superb viewing for thousands of spectators from the steep hillsides which overlook the

After his brilliant second place in Portugal, Ivan Capelli looked for victory in Spain.

117

circuit. Electronic scoreboards. Access tunnels. Restaurants and a giant car park. But hardly anyone goes there — in contrast to the Motor-Cycle GP which attracts a crowd of some 120,000 people. Ah well, all the more room for us I suppose!

Both the two practice days were dry, sunny and hot — about thirty degrees and that's hot! Amidst general complaints about the dirtiness and slipperiness of the track (on account of it being used so little) they confirmed the belief that the normally-aspirated teams were in with an excellent chance of doing well on Sunday. In brilliant form Nigel Mansell was by far the fastest in Friday morning's Free session and although there was yet another all-McLaren front row of the grid (the Team's tenth of 1988) with Ayrton Senna occupying his eleventh pole position of the season and Alain Prost second, Mansell was third only 2/10s slower than Senna's qualifying boost time. With Thierry Boutsen and Alessandro Nannini fourth and fifth in their Benetton-Fords, Capelli sixth in his March-Judd and Patrese seventh in his Williams-Judd there were five 'atmospheric' cars in the top seven. 7/10s covered the fourth to ninth fastest. One second covered the tenth to twentieth and half a second covered the last six. 'This' we said 'is going to be good'! The last time a non-turbo car had won a Grand Prix was at Detroit in 1983 (Michele Alboreto in a Tyrrell-Ford). Were we going to see one win here?

It was hot again on race day. Mansell was fastest in the half hour 'Race Trim' warm-up

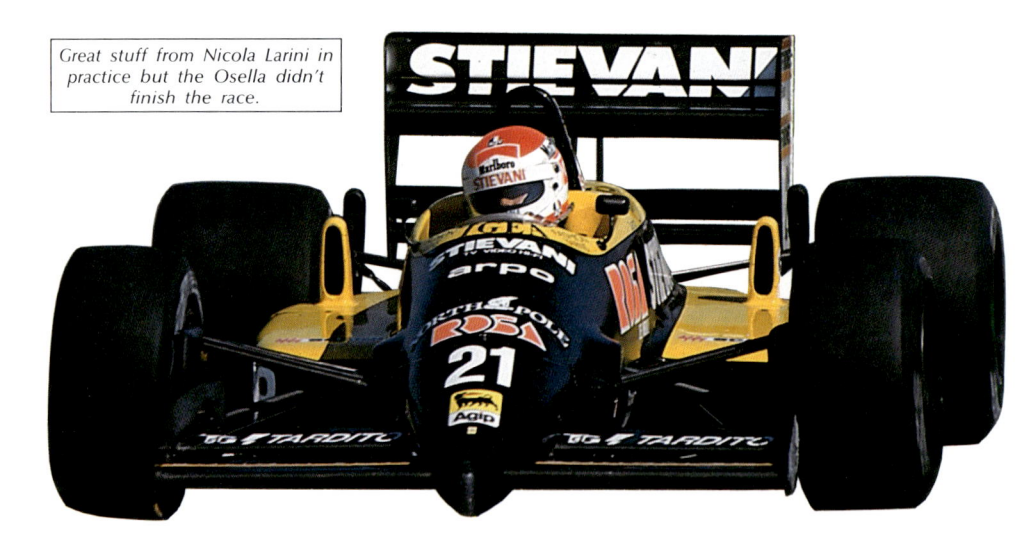

Great stuff from Nicola Larini in practice but the Osella didn't finish the race.

with Boutsen second, Nannini fourth and Gugelmin sixth. Senna and Prost? Fifth and seventh! But what mattered was that they were on the front row of the grid so, given the difficulties of passing at Jerez, they were in a commanding position provided they got away well. 'I'm going to try to separate them at the start' said Mansell 'but failing that I'll aim to sit behind them, hope they race each other and see what develops.'

For once Senna didn't get it right. Prost, repeating all the resolve and determination that he'd shown in Portugal, absolutely shot into the lead immediately followed by Mansell whose start was meteoric. He blasted past Senna to tuck his Williams' nose under Prost's gearbox — exactly what he'd hoped to do. But Alain was even more impressive. At the end of the first lap he was

Race 14 — SPAIN

It didn't matter which way they drove, both Larrauri and Ghinzani failed to make the grid.

nearly two seconds ahead of Nigel with Senna third, Patrese fourth, Capelli fifth, Nannini sixth, Berger seventh and Alboreto a trailing eighth. But in the Benetton team it was Boutsen's turn to strike misfortune as he hit Capelli's March, damaged his nosecone and had to stop for a new one.

'Situation normal' we momentarily thought as Senna powered past Mansell's Williams at the end of the second lap but momentarily it was, for as he ran wide on the exit to the corner Nigel nipped past him on the inside — back into second place. Great stuff! And that was the last that Ayrton saw of his team-mate or Nigel as he fought to stay where he was. Close behind him there was a titanic struggle for fourth place between Patrese, Capelli and Nannini with Berger doing his best to catch it — and all of them gaining on the Brazilian's McLaren.

For twenty-eight riveting laps there was no change to the first seven places. Prost, Mansell, Senna, Patrese, Capelli, Nannini, Berger (Alboreto retired from eighth to be replaced by Piquet on lap sixteen). But at any moment during the 42 minutes those laps took to complete, there could have been! At times Mansell was a mere half second behind a calm but concerned Prost who was cautiously conserving his tyres and fuel. Senna was having to watch his mirrors whilst Capelli was swarming round the rear of the obstructive Patrese's Williams, Nannini was looking for a way past the March and Berger's Ferrari was closing on the battle ahead. It was wonderful to watch.

119

MURRAY WALKER'S GRAND PRIX YEAR

TEAM ANALYSIS

LOTUS
Not much to write home about from Spain. Eighth race out of fourteen with no points. Piquet starts ninth. With diminishing grip takes early tyre stop (lap 31). Rejoins eleventh to be 'held up by Warwick for ten laps'. Delighted to finish eighth after 'a very hard race in a very good car'. Nakajima 15th on grid. Heads long queue for eleventh place but spins out of race, lap 15.

TYRRELL
Both drivers involved in practice altercations with Williams men. Mansell lambasts Palmer for 'getting in the way'. Patrese outrageously 'brake tests' innocent Bailey who non-qualifies for ninth time. Palmer starts 22nd (after being excellent eighth on Friday and ninth in Sunday 'warm up'). Hits Johansson at start. Retires, lap five, with punctured radiator.

WILLIAMS
Excellent race for team marred only by 'Rock Ape' tactics by Patrese in 'brake testing' blameless Julian Bailey during practice (incurring inadequate $10,000 fine from FISA). Mansell absolutely inspired throughout meeting. Qualifies superb third (fastest NA) only 2/10s off pole. Passes Senna at start and then relentlessly chases leader Prost for whole race. For a time only 0.5s behind Alain. In his second finish of 1988 takes second place (as in Britain) with second fastest lap of race (fastest NA) despite sticking clutch and long tyre stop (obstinate wheel nut). Patrese starts seventh and drives gritty non-stop race to finish fifth only 7/10s behind Senna. Both cars in points for first time in 1988.

ZAKSPEED
Team's gloomy forecast in Portugal comes true. Neither Ghinzani (30th) nor Schneider (27th) qualify for race — both complaining of handling and grip deficiencies. 1989 can't come too soon for Zakspeed.

McLAREN
By McLaren's superlative standards only a partly satisfactory race. Tenth grid front-row of '88 with Senna on his eleventh pole of season and Prost second. Prost takes lead at start and stays there in one of the finest races of his career. With need to watch tyres and fuel coolly staves off inspired Mansell to win sixth '88 race and preserve Championship hopes. Also makes fastest lap (Lap 60: 1m 27.845s=107.410mph). Senna has second race running with fuel read-out problem. From pole position passed by Prost, Mansell, Capelli and Nannini before late lap 50 tyre stop. Fights back to finish fourth — running out of fuel as crosses line. Now one win away from Championship with two races to go but Prost has psychological advantage. With thirteen 1988 wins Team McLaren breaks its own 1984 record.

AGS
Streiff qualifies well at 13th. Retires from twelfth, lap 17, with blown engine.

MARCH
Excellent but disappointing race. Capelli and Gugelmin qualify sixth and eleventh after traffic and balance problems. Another storming race drive by Capelli (in spare car after Sunday warm-up throttle slide problem with race car) takes him to brilliant third place past Nannini, Patrese and Senna in spite of no clutch from lap 12. Retires lap 46 (engine). Gugelmin, in first race at Jerez, fights up to fifth by lap 50 but, passed by Senna and Berger, finishes seventh. First time team out of points since French GP.

ARROWS
Four cylinder turbo engine with long throttle lag, bad news at twisty Jerez. After almost every problem imaginable Warwick qualifies 17th and Cheever a disastrous 25th. Warwick up to tenth by lap 38 but then, lap 41 with worn tyres, hits kerb, punctures undertray and retires. Cheever delayed by spinning Palmer lap one. Spins again lap six. After two stops and puncture despondently retires from 16th and last, lap 61, with persistent bottoming.

Mansell — a team effort from a great team brought a super second place.

BENETTON
Amidst general acclamation Team announce that Johnny Herbert will join Nannini in 1989. Boutsen and Nannini qualify well at fourth and fifth (in spite of Boutsen second-fastest Friday time being disallowed for 'too low' front wing end plate). After bad start and early lap 29 tyre stop Nannini storms up from ninth to finish third for the second time in 1988. Boutsen obliged to change nosecone after hitting Capelli, lap one. Rejoins 25th and last. Then drives superlative non-stop race to finish ninth. Benetton now have seven 1988 third places.

Race 14 — SPAIN

Ayrton's fuel gauge a matter for serious thought.

OSELLA
The impressive Nicola Larini qualifies very well at 14th in an unimpressive car. Crashes in Sunday warm-up but races against Nakajima and Streiff in repaired car until retiring from 13th, lap ten, with broken front suspension.

RIAL
De Cesaris qualifies only 23rd after problems with new-type Goodyear rear tyre rubbing against uprights. With appropriate modifications races up to excellent ninth, lap 34, before retiring, lap 38 (engine).

MINARDI
Major handling problems due to new front suspension being incompatible with old rear one. Martini starts 20th and chases De Cesaris for fifteen laps before retiring from 16th, lap 16, with sticky throttle and resultant gearbox malfunction. Sala starts 24th in home GP after crashing twice at Estoril post-race Pirelli tyre testing. Drives steady race towards rear of field to finish twelfth out of fourteen classified (two laps down).

LIGIER
Both drivers qualify — Arnoux 19th and Johansson 21st. 'At Jerez where everyone's got handling problems ours don't show up as much!' Arnoux retires lap one with throttle jammed shut. Johansson hit by Palmer lap one.

Changes nosecone lap three. Then runs last but two until retiring, lap 63, with wheel on point of dropping off. 1988 really has been a character-building year for Stefan — and Ligier.

FERRARI
Dismal practice sees Berger eighth on grid ('traffic') and Alboreto tenth ('throttle response'). Gerhard runs seventh for 28 laps in five car train battling for third behind Senna, Patrese, Capelli, Nannini. Tyre stop lap 29. Rejoins ninth and progresses to finish sixth — running out of fuel at last corner. Alboreto, still without drive for 1989, trails in eighth place until lap 16 when retires with engine water leak.

LOLA
Alliot crashes race car on Saturday. Qualifies 12th in spare. Races strongly in tenth place for ten laps. Then has to pit for new front wheel after original cut through by obstruction between brake caliper and rim! Rejoins one from last but soldiers on to finish fourteenth, last classified, three laps down. Dalmas starts sixteenth for first Jerez race and has uneventful drive to eleventh (one lap down).

COLONI
Tarquini fails to pre-qualify due to broken throttle cable and fuel pump failure.

EUROBRUN
For the seventh time in last eight meetings Larrauri fails to qualify. After crashing race car on Friday Modena just gets spare on to grid at 26th. Then uses his wasted talent to force inadequate car to 13th place (two laps down).

DALLARA
Caffi manages to qualify 18th in spite of two days sickness leaving him weak and listless. Drives now-expected excellent race. Up to tenth, laps 16 to 30, behind Piquet and Gugelmin and ahead of Warwick. Then to eighth lap 31. Exhaust pipe breaks (again) causing loss of two places to finish tenth (one lap down). Talented Dallara Designer Sergio Rinland being propositioned by rival teams for 1989 (rumours say he will join reconstituted Brabham team with Alboreto and Alfa V10 engine!)

It's a long way from the back of the pack to the victory rostrum.

On lap 29 the predicted tyre changes started. In came Nannini for a new set of Goodyear 'boots'. An early move which turned out to be the right one for Alessandro who dropped from sixth to ninth but who immediately began to gain places on his new and grippier rubber. Lap thirty and in came Gerhard Berger who also dropped from sixth to ninth — as did Nelson Piquet when he stopped on lap thirty-one. But the men ahead — Prost, Mansell, Senna, Patrese and Capelli — showed no sign of stopping yet. We were watching an enthralling tactical battle where anything could happen and probably would.

Especially as Cappelli was on his way! With Prost speeding up to widen the gap between himself and Mansell to nearly five seconds Ivan, after ninety-one miles of unremitting effort, finally found a way round Patrese's wide Williams and moved up to fourth on lap 36. Three laps later at exactly the same place, the hairpin before the pit straight, he did the same thing to Senna! Twice in two races the spectacular March-Man had blown off Ayrton's McLaren — and made it look easy, eventually! Prost led, Mansell second, Capelli third, Senna fourth, Patrese fifth and a charging Nannini back to sixth with the fastest lap of the race so far (1m 28.57s). So now, on the edges of our seats, we relished the possibility of Capelli catching Prost and Mansell and even the chance of that longed-for 3½ litre win. But it was not to be for on lap 46, with a smoking Judd behind him, Ivan pulled on to the side of the track to retire after another outstanding drive that had emphasised his brilliance and that of his car's designer, Adrian Newey.

The outstanding Nannini gets ready to pounce on Gugelmin, Patrese and Senna.

Race 14 — SPAIN

Stefan actually had a motor race in Spain!

Just one lap later Mansell's chances of increasing his GP wins to fourteen were destroyed when a sticking wheel nut at his tyre stop put Prost beyond his reach. He rejoined without losing his second place — an indication of how much of a lead he had built over Senna, now back in third place after Capelli's retirement. But Ayrton wasn't to stay there for long. Nannini who'd had such bad luck at the two previous races, was really flying on his new tyres. On lap 48 he not only passed Patrese to fourth but Senna to third! 3½ litre cars second (Mansell) and third (Nannini) with Patrese fifth and right up with Senna! And on lap 51 Ayrton was out of the points down to seventh with Patrese, Gugelmin and Berger ahead of him as he stopped for new tyres. Now the title was wide-open for Ayrton had to finish at least fourth if he was to clinch the Championship with just one more win. Grimly he set about passing Berger, Gugelmin and Patrese to get there. Lap 55 — past Gugelmin (who'd been taken by Berger). Lap 58 — past the Ferrari. Fourteen laps to go and Patrese, driving a non-stop race, was a long way ahead! But with non-stop Riccardo slithering around the track on shot tyres, Senna remorselessly closed on the Williams. And on lap 65 he passed it — up to the fourth place needed.

But Prost won. His sixth victory of 1988, the 34th of his magnificent career and the fastest lap of the race (lap 60: 1m 27.845=107.410mph) to underline his effortless superiority. With Nigel Mansell an equally magnificent second (his second second-place of the year in only two finishes) having again demonstrated that when it comes to guts and dogged determination he is second to none. Nannini a superb third (his second of 1988 and another indication that he is a superstar in the making). Senna a very fed-up fourth having again had a faulty fuel read-out and having run out as he crossed the line, Patrese a gritty fifth and Berger an almost fuel-less sixth.

Well we may not have had that elusive first 3½ litre win but we certainly had a race! And now, knowing that he had been conclusively beaten by Prost in the last two races, Ayrton Senna had a worrying month ahead of him until the Japanese Grand Prix which would give him the World Championship he so desperately wanted — if he won. Or could keep Prost's chances alive if he didn't!

MURRAY WALKER'S GRAND PRIX YEAR

'French without tears' — Alain Prost and Philippe Alliot take the stage.

SPANISH GRAND PRIX

Winner: Alain Prost, McLaren-Honda MP4/4-06 **Fastest Lap:** Alain Prost, 107.345 mph

GRID POSITION		RESULTS			WORLD CHAMPIONSHIP			
No.	Driver	Pos.	Driver	Car	Drivers	Pts	Constructors	Pts
12	Senna	1	Prost	McLaren-Honda MP4/4-06	1. Prost	84*	1. McLaren-Honda	169
11	Prost	2	Mansell	Williams-Judd FW12/1	2. Senna	79	2. Ferrari	62
5	Mansell	3	Nannini	Benetton-Ford B188-07	3. Berger	38	3. Benetton-Ford	38
20	Boutsen	4	Senna	McLaren-Honda MP4/4-05	4. Boutsen	25	4. Arrows-Megatron	20
19	Nannini	5	Patrese	Williams-Judd FW12/3	5. Alboreto	24	5. March-Judd	19
16	Capelli	6	Berger	Ferrari F187/88C-103	6. Piquet	16	6. Lotus-Honda	17
6	Patrese	7	Gugelmin	March-Judd 881/2	7. Warwick	15	7. Williams-Judd	16
28	Berger	8	Piquet	Lotus-Honda 100T/2	8. Capelli	14	8. Tyrrell-Cosworth	5
1	Piquet	9	Boutsen	Benetton-Ford B188-05	9. Nannini	13	9. Rial-Cosworth	3
27	Alboreto	10	Caffi	Dallara-Cosworth F188/003	10. Mansell	12	10. Minardi-Cosworth	1
15	Gugelmin	11	Dalmas	Lola-Cosworth LC88-03	11. Cheever	5		
30	Alliot	12	Sala	Minardi-Cosworth M188-02	Gugelmin	5		
14	Streiff	13	Modena	EuroBrun-Cosworth 188-01	Palmer	5		
21	Larini	14	Alliot	Lola-Cosworth LC88-1	14. Patrese	4		
2	Nakajima				15. De Cesaris	3		
29	Dalmas				16. Martini	1		
17	Warwick				Nakajima	1		
36	Caffi							
25	Arnoux							
23	Martini				*Points total counting best 11 results only.			
26	Johansson							
3	Palmer							
22	De Cesaris							
24	Sala							
18	Cheever							
33	Modena							

Ayrton Senna World Champion 1988

31st October 1988
Circuit: Suzuka

Japan

'UP to now the Portuguese Grand Prix of 1985, when I won in the wet, was my best race — but this one was better. I have lost a great weight from my shoulders. It was a very hard race — I was very lucky and I am very pleased. I have won the World Championship thanks to being in the right team for the first time and I would like to thank McLaren and Honda for the big improvement in my car over the last two races.'

So said a justifiably jubilant Ayrton Senna immediately after what was the most exciting race of the season and which ensured that the right man won Motor Racing's highest honour — the one who had scored the most points by winning the most races. And it was fitting that it happened at the Suzuka circuit, the property of Honda who had provided the near-invincible power that had taken Senna to the 1988 Drivers' World Championship.

It was only the second Grand Prix that had been held at the superb track near Nagoya and, as in 1987, half Nippon seemed to be there. Hardly surprising for the 120,000-plus spectators from motorsport-mad Japan knew that it was their event that would decide whether Ayrton Senna would achieve his single-minded ambition to become the first new World Champion since 1985 or whether his equally determined team-mate Alain Prost would keep himself in the running for his third Championship in four years. The situation could not have been simpler — both had to win to achieve their objective and neither was going to defer to the other. So the prospects were for something very special and they were realised — but not in a way that anyone could have foreseen.

The drivers like Suzuka. Its 3.7 mile lap is unique in that its distorted 'Figure of Eight' outline accommodates an underpass and a bridge. It has just about every kind of corner, including a sixty mile an hour first gear hairpin, and it has gradient. The surface is really grippy and the facilities are excellent.

At last! A real smile from Ayrton Senna.

1987 had seen a literally shocking result for Japan: the loss of face was massive when Gerhard Berger's Ferrari won on Honda's home ground. During qualifying for the 1988 race a repeat of this demeaning defeat seemed unlikely to say the least, but amazingly it was to look possible, in what was to be an absolutely riveting race.

No great surprises in practice but there were some interesting situations. Once again (for the eleventh time) it was the 'Red and Whites' on the front row of the grid. Senna in pole position for a record twelfth time and Prost next, $^3/_{10}$s slower. So nothing

125

Sickness overwhelmed the outgoing World Champion — out at two-thirds distance.

in it — especially as Alain had missed a gear on his 'hot' lap. Berger was third and that was no novelty either. But then, fourth on the grid, was the top atmospheric driver, the ebullient Ivan Capelli in his March-Judd, generating thoughts that if Senna and Prost pushed each other so hard that their fuel consumption suffered, Ivan might well be up front at the end. With an appropriate 'Banzai' effort Satoru Nakajima was sixth, next to his team-mate Piquet, at the circuit he knew better than any of the others. Nigel Mansell was a disappointed eighth after his great achievement in Spain, and there was a newcomer in twentieth place — Japan's Aguri Suzuki substituting for Yannick Dalmas in the Lola team as a result of the Frenchman having contracted a severe ear infection the week before.

At the start of the 51 lap race, in dull conditions and on a still damp track after earlier rain, Alain Prost must have thought it was Christmas. For, with a perfect start, he shot past Senna who just sat there! 'It was the only start I missed and it was the one I needed most,' said Ayrton. Not once but

A very eventful race for Alboreto — spins, battles and a punch-up with Nannini.

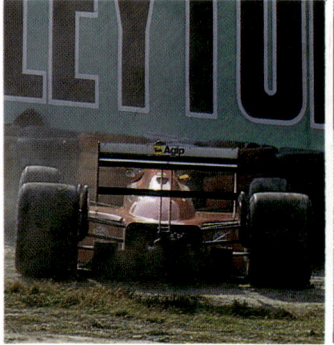

Stefan Johansson didn't qualify but happily provided a taxi service for Gerhard Berger.

Race 15 — JAPAN

Senna's incredible 'charge' — from 14th at the start, to a victorious lead on lap 27, and the 1988 World Championship.

twice the bow-string taut Brazilian stalled his engine. It was only his good luck that he had some momentum, and that the Suzuka start line is on a slope, that enabled him to drop the clutch and 'bump' his Honda V6 into life. By the time he had done so he was down in fourteenth place — but not for long! At the end of the first lap, with Prost leading, Berger second and Capelli a close third followed at a distance by Alboreto, Boutsen, Nannini and Patrese, Ayrton was up to eighth — and flying! But into the pits came Mansell for a new nosecone to replace the one that had been ripped off when he tried to pass the fast-starting, fourth-placed, Derek Warwick who also furiously pitted with a puncture as a result of the impact.

Senna may have been late getting away but from then on his driving was nothing short of sensational. Using to the full all his immense skill, incisiveness and experience he awe-inspiringly overwhelmed the opposition. Past Patrese and Nannini to sixth on lap two. Past Boutsen on lap three. And into a gap which hadn't looked to be there to take fourth from Alboreto on lap four. Only Prost, Berger and Capelli to catch now but with Alain some ten seconds ahead victory seemed to be a vain hope. For now the amazing Ivan Capelli was not only the fastest man on the track (1m 46.58s = 120.7 mph) but was right up with Berger. And on lap five the turquoise Leyton House March-Judd was past the scarlet Ferrari with Gerhard already worried about fuel consumption. Great stuff!

With action like this at the front there weren't a lot of eyes for what was happening behind, but there was plenty going on there too. Like Alboreto, with unintended assistance from Alessandro Nannini, spinning out of sixth place into the deep

TEAM ANALYSIS

LOTUS
Good practice but poor race for both drivers. After feeling unwell on Friday, Piquet qualifies fifth with Nakajima excellent sixth on exactly same time as Nelson. Piquet down to tenth, lap one, after avoiding stationary Senna at start. Seventh by lap seven but then, with reduced concentration due to feeling sick, spins off lap ten. Rejoins after pits check but retires, lap 35, with sickness after being hit by Mansell. Nakajima stalls at start but fights through field to finish seventh.

TYRRELL
With big improvements to car incorporating 1989 components both drivers qualify for the first time since Silverstone. Palmer 16th after many problems and Bailey 26th. In heavyweight spare car 'better than it has been all season' Palmer up to excellent eighth by lap twelve. Then delayed by puncture but still finishes twelfth (one lap down). Bailey has satisfying race to finish 14th (two laps down).

WILLIAMS
Another fruitless Japanese trip for Mansell. Starts eighth after going off on fast lap. In fifth place hits Warwick on lap one and pits for new nosecone. Climbs to twelfth but then retires after colliding with lapped Piquet when trying to pass on lap 25. Patrese gains four places on lap one from eleventh on grid. Then, with acute understeer, improves to sixth, lap 20, and goes full distance to finish there.

ZAKSPEED
25 kg weight reduction to cars since Jerez. Ghinzani again fails to qualify. Schneider starts 25th after heavy off in practice. Vigorously improves to good 16th by lap 13 but then obliged to retire with numb arm after Friday shunt.

McLAREN
Senna starts from record twelfth 1988 pole position with Prost again second on grid. Ayrton twice stalls engine at start and gets away fourteenth. Then drives inspired recovery race to catch and pass leader Prost on lap 27. With fastest lap of race (lap 33: 1m 46.326 = 123.266 mph) wins eighth Grand Prix of season (record) by seven seconds and takes World Championship with record score of 87 points (with a race still to go). Prost leads for 26 laps hotly pursued and briefly passed by sensational Capelli. Wrestles with faulty gearbox until, with additional problems of traffic and wet/dry track, concedes victory. Finishes second in race and Championship. Seemingly no records now left for team to beat!

AGS
Encouraging race for the little French team decimated by personnel defections. Streiff starts 18th and races strongly to highest finish of season — eighth (one lap down) after terrific scrap with Alliot.

MARCH
Excellent but very disappointing race for the ever-improving Bicester team. In their Leyton House sponsor's home country, Ivan Capelli qualifies superb fourth and Gugelmin 13th (with Friday time as a result of major Saturday accident). Capelli sensational in race. Passes Berger Ferrari to second, lap 5, and then catches leader Prost. Briefly takes lead on lap 15 to become first NA driver to head a GP for four years. Forced to retire from second, lap 20, with electrical problem (car fires first time after race ...!). Gugelmin, dangerously hampered for whole distance by loose drink bottle fouling pedals, drives courageous race to finish tenth.

The brilliant Capelli became the first atmospheric driver to lead a Grand Prix for four years — albeit for only 200 metres!

ARROWS
Warwick qualifies well at seventh. Up to fourth after start but rammed by Mansell. Furiously into pits with rear tyre puncture. Rejoins only to spin off, lap 17, and retire when four laps down. Cheever beset by, mainly engine, problems all through practice. Qualifies 15th with Friday time. Runs eighth laps 21 to 38 before retiring, lap 39, with turbo fire.

BENETTON
Poor qualifying achievements by both drivers due to traffic problems and surprising lack of grip. Boutsen starts tenth and Nannini twelfth. Thierry then drives usual unobtrusively impressive race to finish third (top NA) for the sixth time in 1988 (record) and consolidate fourth place in Championship. Nannini has eventful race. Alboreto refuses to yield, lap eight, when challenged for sixth. Resultant contact causes Alboreto to spin out. Later, when lapped, Michele again baulks Nannini who then loses fourth place to Berger. Post-race 'discussion' leads to Italian punch-up. Nevertheless both Benettons satisfyingly finish in points.

OSELLA
As usual the competent Larini's story is, sadly, quickly told. 24th on the grid in his tired and ineffective Osella and retirement on lap 35 with a sick engine and loose front wheel nut.

Race 15 — JAPAN

The nearest Warwick's Arrows came to 'flying' all weekend.

RIAL
It is just as well that De Cesaris is leaving for his sixth team (Dallara) in 1989. To the wrath of the irascible Rial owner, Gunther Schmid, Andrea writes off yet another car on Friday ('but it wasn't my fault') prior to going into the wall in the spare on Saturday. Still qualifies 14th. In eleventh place deliberately crowds new-boy Suzuki to standstill to 'punish' him for getting in his way. Later blamed for baulking Prost and enabling Senna to take lead. Retires, lap 27, with overheating — not before time.

MINARDI
Both drivers start and both finish. Martini qualifies 17th and Sala 22nd. Uneventful race for both (except for short-lived Sala misfire) with Pierluigi finishing 17th (two laps down) and Luis 15th (also minus two laps).

LIGIER
Revised front suspension and new front wing and nose result in improved times at Imola testing but for the sixth time Stefan Johansson fails to qualify due to 'no grip'. With different settings to Stefan, René Arnoux gets in at 23rd. Runs at rear of field to take last classified place, 17th, (three laps down).

FERRARI
Berger again qualifies third, one and a half seconds off Senna's pole time, with usual gloomy prophesies about inevitable fuel consumption problem in race. Which are then fulfilled as he eases off to drop to fifth after running second to Prost for first five laps. With help from team-mate Alboreto, passes Nannini four laps from end to finish fourth. Alboreto starts ninth after engine problems. Fourth in early laps. Inadvertently nudged out of sixth and into sand by Nannini on lap seven. Regains track to finish eleventh (one lap down) after again baulking Nannini. Spirited post-race discussion leads to rough-house between the two Italians.

LOLA
Japanese Formula 3000 driver Aguri Suzuki makes last moment substitution for Dalmas as result of Yannick having ear infection. With no pre-practice experience of car, Suzuki qualifies superbly at 20th only one place lower and $4/_{ths}$ slower than team-mate Alliot. Then races well despite two spins and being 'disciplined' to a standstill by De Cesaris to finish 16th (three laps down). From 19th on grid Alliot gains six places on first lap and in aggressively competent race, takes creditable ninth (one lap down) — highest place of season.

COLONI
Tarquini again fails to pre-qualify. 'Nothing wrong with the car — it's just too slow.'

EUROBRUN
With engine and gearbox problems in a car which is already not up to it both Larrauri and Modena again fail to qualify.

DALLARA
Team depressed by knowledge that Designer Sergio Rinland is to join a revived Brabham team in 1989. Alex Caffi starts 21st after multiple engine problems. Retires from 17th place after hitting wall on lap 23.

Aguri Suzuki — an impressive debut for Lola and 16th place.

129

sand on the tricky Spoon Curve! So with Boutsen now fifth, Nannini sixth and Piquet seventh, closer and closer and closer to Prost got Capelli and closer and closer to Berger got Senna. This was, at last, the edge-of-the-seat race for victory that everyone had yearned for during 1988 — with three turbo and three 3½ litre cars contesting the points places. Lap eleven: Piquet into the sand and then the pits and Senna up to third past Berger. Then, three laps later the weather did the Brazilian a favour as it started to rain; Ayrton is supreme in the wet.

But now the man of the moment was Ivan Capelli. On a historic lap fifteen, with greater momentum out of the chicane which leads into the main straight, he ripped past Prost into the lead — the first time that a normally-aspirated car had headed a Grand Prix for four years. Needless to say Alain didn't like that and with a surging blast of extra boost he was back in front by the end of the straight. The next four laps were the best we'd seen for the whole season as Prost, wrestling with a faulty gearbox, fought for the win he had to have to stay in the Championship, with Capelli looming large in his mirrors, Senna right behind the March and Boutsen, now up to fourth past Berger, only a few lengths away.

I suppose it was too good to last and it didn't for on lap 20, to a giant groan of dismay, Capelli fell away, victim of an electrical fault. The end of a magnificent, fighting drive that had thrilled millions of people worldwide. So now Senna was second with the scent of victory in his nostrils and Boutsen was in his 'usual' third place ahead of a massive struggle for fourth between Berger and Nannini. And Prost was in trouble. With his errant gearbox that was making him miss 'at least two changes a lap', with traffic that he freely admits deters him more than it does Senna, and with an on-off wet/dry surface as the rain came and went it wasn't long before a charging Ayrton was closely contemplating his team-mate's gearbox. On lap 27 it happened. As the two McLarens, now as one, came up to lap De Cesaris, Gugelmin and Nakajima, Senna saw the opportunity he had been waiting for. With no room to spare he was past Alain and, as the Frenchman was delayed by the Rial, he broke clear. With a succession of blinding laps, including the fastest of the race (lap 33: 1m 46.326s = 123.27 mph) he built a lead of over three seconds and although Prost got it down to less that two whilst Senna was trying to lap Nakajima he, in his own words, 'gave up' when the rain returned and Senna pulled away again — agitatedly gesticulating for the race to be stopped because of the danger of driving with slick tyres on the now wet track. 'I'm

Honda were not the only Japanese company to make their mark — Leyton House had some stylish 'Marchers'.

not disappointed to have lost the Championship. I knew it was going to be difficult. Today reflected the season and Ayrton deserved to win,' Prost generously conceded afterwards, 'but I am very disapppointed at the way the race went. I had no fuel worries and thought I was controlling things well, but with the problems of my gearbox and the traffic I decided not to take risks for the Championship. It was better for myself and for Honda to settle for second.' For his part Senna, strongly supported by Prost, condemned the obstructiveness of the backmarkers. 'They all knew that Alain and I were fighting for the Championship and I expected them to be nicer about letting us by — but no!'

So ended a thrilling and totally absorbing Japanese Grand Prix with Thierry Boutsen

The superb Suzuka Circuit, enormous crowds, and a Honda victory were a great advertisement for Japanese motor racing.

MURRAY WALKER'S GRAND PRIX YEAR

taking his almost customary third place (the sixth time he had done so and yet another all-time record), Berger regaining fourth position after Nannini had been 'delayed' by Alboreto (who, I remind you, had been nudged off by Alessandro earlier!) and Riccardo Patrese taking the last point. With his eighth win of the season, Senna had broken the previous record shared by Jim Clark, Alain Prost and himself. His 87 Championship scoring points were a massive fourteen higher than the previous best (Prost '85 and Piquet '87) with a race still to go and he now very much had the psychological edge over Prost. A very satisfying day's work!

But brilliant as Senna's drive had been, his thoroughly deserved glory was shared by Ivan Capelli. Grand Prix racing is full of 'ifs' but if his March had kept running, there could well have been a different result in Japan. And now, with the knowledge that the street circuit at Adelaide was going to be far more suitable for his March-Judd than Suzuka had been, Ivan was really looking forward to the Australian Grand Prix in two weeks' time!

Diminutive Alain Prost? Blown-up out of proportion? The real thing is much more modest.

JAPANESE GRAND PRIX

Winner: Ayrton Senna, McLaren-Honda MP4/4-05   **Fastest Lap:** Ayrton Senna, 123.266 mph

GRID POSITION			RESULTS			WORLD CHAMPIONSHIP			
No.	Driver	Pos.	Driver	Car	Drivers	Pts	Constructors		Pts
12	Senna	1	Senna	McLaren-Honda MP4/4-05	1. Senna	87*	1. McLaren-Honda		184
11	Prost	2	Prost	McLaren-Honda MP4/4-06	2. Prost	84*	2. Ferrari		65
28	Berger	3	Boutsen	Benetton-Ford B188-08	3. Berger	41	3. Benetton-Ford		44
16	Capelli	4	Berger	Ferrari F187/88C-104	4. Boutsen	29	4. Arrows-Megatron		20
1	Piquet	5	Nannini	Benetton-Ford B188-07	5. Alboreto	24	5. March-Judd		19
2	Nakajima	6	Patrese	Williams-Judd FW12/3	6. Piquet	16	6. Lotus-Honda		17
17	Warwick	7	Nakajima	Lotus-Honda 100T/1	7. Nannini	15	7. Williams-Judd		17
5	Mansell	8	Streiff	AGS-Cosworth JH23/3	Warwick	15	8. Tyrrell-Cosworth		5
27	Alboreto	9	Alliot	Lola-Cosworth LC88-03	9. Capelli	14	9. Rial-Cosworth		3
20	Boutsen	10	Gugelmin	March-Judd 881/6	10. Mansell	12	10. Minardi-Cosworth		1
6	Patrese	11	Alboreto	Ferrari F187/88C-103	11. Cheever	5			
19	Nannini	12	Palmer	Tyrrell-Cosworth DG/017-5	Gugelmin	5			
15	Gugelmin	13	Martini	Minardi-Cosworth M188-05	Palmer	5			
22	De Cesaris	14	Bailey	Tyrrell-Cosworth DG/017-3	Patrese	5			
18	Cheever	15	Sala	Minardi-Cosworth M188-04	15. De Cesaris	3			
3	Palmer	16	Suzuki	Lola-Cosworth LC88-04	16. Martini	1			
23	Martini	17	Arnoux	Ligier-Judd JS31/02	Nakajima	1			
14	Streiff								
30	Alliot								
29	Suzuki				*Points total counting best 11 results only.*				
36	Caffi								
24	Sala								
25	Arnoux								
21	Larini								
10	Schneider								
4	Bailey								

13th October 1988
Circuit: Adelaide

Australia

IF any other country than Australia was allocated the last Grand Prix of the year, there would be massive gloom and despondency in the world of Formula One. Not many of us would be lucky enough to go 'down-under' if it wasn't for the World Championship and the experience of doing so is so enjoyable that it makes a wonderful climax to what, by Round 16, has been a demanding seven months of virtually non-stop activity.

It was not until 1985, thirty-five years after the World Championship was initiated, that Australia became one of the countries visited by the series but right from its inception the race at Adelaide took off like a rocket and it has never looked back. No wonder, because it has everything — a delightful city with the finest street circuit in the Grand Prix world, relaxed but hyper-efficient organisation and administration, the friendly, cheerful, and enthusiastic backing and support of what appears to be the whole of Australia — and a climate which, to people who have just left a grey, winter-imminent Europe, makes South Australia seem like the promised land.

So everyone is more than delighted to be there — and this year, there was an especially stimulating atmosphere. The Championship had been decided so there would be no pressure to drive for points, but with a raft of 'lasts' a lot of the teams and drivers had got plenty to motivate them.

Adelaide was to host the last Grand Prix for the dominant turbo cars which had made their first appearance in 1977. So McLaren and Lotus were to make a final appearance with their devastatingly effective V6 Honda turbo engines. Australia was also to hear the swansong of the Ferrari V6 turbo, the Megatron and Zakspeed fours and the venerable Alfa-Romeo/Osella V8. Of the top drivers, Nigel Mansell was having his last drive for Williams, Alboreto for Ferrari and Boutsen for Benetton. And it was all to happen at the race generally acknowledged to be the toughest of them all. Adelaide's 2.3 mile lap with its twists and turns, five second-gear corners and 180 mph Brabham straight is a hard one — especially demanding on brakes, transmissions and fuel consumption. Eighty-two times round it takes nearly two hours and in 90 degree heat it wasn't going to take many prisoners — only eight finished in 1987!

A record 304,000 sun-drenched Aussies invaded the circuit during the four-day meeting and they had their money's-worth. Under cloudless skies and a blazing sun in 37 °C heat, they saw a thrilling battle for pole on Friday with Prost and Senna alternating for the honour lap by lap. Senna took a record 13th premier grid position of the season in the closing seconds of the session with Prost a mere $^1/_{10}$ of a second behind him. So they were starting even. With an inspired Nigel Mansell third (and the leading 'atmospheric' driver) ahead of Berger's Ferrari, Piquet's Lotus-Honda and his team-mate Patrese's Williams, the sparks were clearly going to fly on Sunday — and they did!

It was cooler for the race — only 30°! — and Alain got it absolutely right at the start. Straight into the lead immediately to pull away from Senna with Berger and Piquet, exploiting their superior turbo power, blasting past Mansell into third and fourth. At the end of the lap Prost led Senna by an amazing 2.1 seconds, with Berger snapping at the Brazilian's gearbox. On lap four Alain was 5½ seconds ahead but now it was Berger

133

MURRAY WALKER'S GRAND PRIX YEAR

Nice one Philippe! (Again).

Oh Nelson! Right in front of the Stag Hotel crowd too.

Race 16 — AUSTRALIA

Poor Piercarlo Ghinzani must have driven more races for less points than anyone else.

Ayrton Senna — now definitely one of the all-time greats.

With legs like that who needs a Grand Prix?

TEAM ANALYSIS

LOTUS
A heartening season's end for Team Lotus in its last race with Honda power after announcing that Nakajima had re-signed for '89 and that Frank Dernie will be the team's new designer. Piquet qualifies fifth and races to his third third-place of 1988 to finish a lacklustre sixth in Drivers' Championship. Nakajima, no lover of street circuits, starts 13th. Retires on lap 28 after hitting Gugelmin in four-car incident started by Martini spin. Lotus takes unimpressive fourth place in Constructors' Championship.

TYRRELL
Jonathan Palmer (fourth in 1987) starts 17th in spare car with revised '1989' front suspension after thumping wall in final Sunday practice. Holds 16th place for 15 laps before retiring, lap 17, with broken transmission. Shares twelfth place in championship with Cheever and Gugelmin. A thoroughly disheartened Julian Bailey fails to qualify for the tenth time. Team Tyrrell eighth in Constructors' Championship.

Riccardo and Nigel thrilled us all for 65 laps.

WILLIAMS
Revised bodywork and suspension for final race with Judd engines. In his last meeting as a Williams' driver Nigel Mansell qualifies strong third (fastest NA) with Patrese an excellent sixth on grid for his record-equalling 176th GP. Patrese/Mansell pursue Piquet for fourth/third place for 65 laps. Patrese spins, lap 52, and Mansell retires from fourth, lap 66, when brakes fail. Riccardo finishes in praiseworthy best-of-'88 fourth place. Mansell tenth in championship and Patrese 11th. Williams fifth equal with Arrows/March in Constructors' Championship.

ZAKSPEED
Last race with own unsuccessful turbo motor before switching to Yamaha power for '89. Schneider, still troubled by Japanese GP practice arm strain, does not qualify for tenth time. After spinning twice Ghinzani retires from 12th and last place, lap 70, with broken fuel pump.

McLAREN
A superb end to a magnificent season. For last race with Honda turbo motor Senna takes record 13th pole of season with strapped wrist after Bali holiday mishap. Prost second on grid for 12th 1988 McLaren front row. After Berger lap 26 retirement from lead Prost dominates race to win second Australian and seventh '88 GP with fastest lap (lap 59: 1m 21.216s = 103.870 mph) and score record 105 total points. Slowed by defective gearbox Senna finishes second for tenth 1988 McLaren clean sweep. After unprecedently successful season McLaren win Constructors' Championship with staggering 199 points. Senna World Champion with record 90 'best 11 races' points and Prost second with 87.

Adelaide was heartening for Streiff and AGS.

AGS
Streiff starts 16th using much improved Jean Silani-designed rear suspension. With top priority to finish does so in eleventh place as last classified driver after stopping nine laps short with electrical failure when seventh.

MARCH
A disappointing Australia following recent outstanding successes. After practice handling problems for both drivers, Capelli starts ninth and 'first time' Gugelmin 19th. Capelli drives gritty race to finish sixth (one lap down) in spite of poor handling, brake problems, no clutch from half-distance, losing front rubbing strip after hitting debris, and a rear puncture! Also achieves fastest NA lap (lap 69: 1m 21.526s) only $^3/_{10}$s slower than Prost's fastest of race. Gugelmin similarly affected. Tyres too hot. Poor handling. No clutch after ten laps. Hit by Nakajima in four-car incident, lap 47, and retires. Capelli seventh-equal in championship. Gugelmin twelfth-equal. March fifth-equal in Constructors' Championship.

Race 16 — AUSTRALIA

ARROWS
Unrewarding end to encouraging season. For his 100th GP and last with Megatron turbo engine Warwick starts good seventh. Ninth/tenth until lap 53 retirement (engine). Finishes seventh equal in Championship. After endless engine problems in practice Cheever starts 18th in spare car. Retires from 13th, lap 50 (engine). Takes 12th equal in Championship. In 11th season of GP racing Arrows take highest-ever Constructors' Championship fifth-equal place.

BENETTON
A poor end to a very good year. After practice car-balance and traffic problems Nannini and Boutsen start eighth (third NA) and tenth. Nannini spins down to 13th, lap 17. Spins again in eleventh place, lap 64, and cannot restart. 'No grip' Boutsen spins, lap 15, but finishes fifth (one lap down) in spite of high speed misfire and broken exhaust. After excellent season Boutsen highest NA driver in Championship at fourth. Nannini seventh equal. With a finish in every GP (only team to do so), eight podium and thirteen points places, Benetton finish satisfying third and top NA team in Constructors' Championship.

OSELLA
Let down yet again by his outmoded Alfa-Romeo/Osella engine Nicola Larini fails to pre-qualify. A 24,000 mile return trip for only five laps at Adelaide!

RIAL
An encouraging but disappointing Australian trip. For his last Rial race Andrea de Cesaris qualifies 15th after a customary two days of problems. Drives excellent race to advance to strong fifth place on lap 66. Then runs out of fuel. Classified eighth, one lap down. Fifteenth in Drivers' Championship.

MINARDI
Martini equals best-yet grid position at 14th. Despite clutch and electrical problems races to creditable seventh place (two laps down) and finishes 16th equal in Championship with one point. Sala qualifies 21st. Retires from 16th out of 20, lap 45 (engine). Thanks to Ford-power Minardi finish best-yet tenth in Constructors' Championship.

LIGIER
Both drivers qualify for Team's 200th GP with exhortations from Guy Ligier to finish. Only Stefan does so. In last race with Judd-power Arnoux starts 23rd and collides with leader Berger when being lapped (lap 26). After qualifying 22nd Johansson doggedly achieves seventh place team needs for 1989 'free travel' entitlement (saving of some $2m!) only to run out of fuel when in points at sixth five laps from end. Classified ninth (four laps down). A disastrous season for Ligier with no points scored.

FERRARI
Last turbo race for Ferrari. Last Ferrari race for Alboreto. Berger (pole and winner in '87) qualifies fourth. Despite certainty of running out of fuel Gerhard spectacularly goes for broke. Third lap one. Second lap three. Past Prost to the lead lap 14. Then 12 glorious laps heading the field until lap 26 collision-into-retirement with Arnoux's Ligier. For Alboreto a miserable end to his mixed-fortune five season Ferrari career. Twelfth on the grid and first lap race retirement after being hit by Caffi. Berger takes distant third in Drivers' Championship. Alboreto an even more distant fifth. Ferrari second in Constructors' Championship — 134 points behind McLaren!

LOLA
Formula One new-boy Pierre-Henri Raphanel unsuccessfully attempts to qualify for first GP in place of absent Yannick Dalmas (Legionnaire's Disease). After multiple-offs, Alliot starts 24th. Races at tail of field to finish tenth, five laps down, after running out of fuel.

Pierre-Henri Raphanel failed to qualify for his first GP.

COLONI
In a car which looks good but goes slow Tarquini fails to qualify.

EUROBRUN
Both drivers qualify for the first time since Germany (race 9). Modena 20th, Larrauri 25th. After starting from back of grid Modena repeatedly spins before retiring from 14th out of 15, lap 64 (broken driveshaft). Larrauri retires from tail end of field, lap 12 (driveshaft). Bernie Ecclestone announces that Walter Brun has bought entire Brabham assets...

DALLARA
Another impressive performance puts Alex Caffi 11th on the grid. Punts Alboreto into retirement lap one. Ninth laps 17-20. Retires from tenth, lap 33 (clutch).

second as a result of audaciously passing Senna on the inside of the second-gear Racetrack Hairpin. And now we saw one of the most aggressively determined drives of 1988. Gerhard Berger knew (and so did Prost) that unless he let his fuel read-out rule his heart he wouldn't finish the race. But this was the last race of the year and the very last turbo Grand Prix so, the hell with it, he was going to go down with all guns blazing! Yard by spell-binding yard, he positively exploded round Adelaide on the razor's edge between adhesion and disaster until, on lap 14, having destroyed Prost's comfortable cushion, he passed Alain at the same place he'd taken Senna. Ferrari leads! Nine laps later, he led by three seconds as he came up to lap Stefano Modena and René Arnoux — and prematurely finish the race he'd won the previous year. As Gerhard slipped inside the Ligier, Arnoux, unsighted by Modena, turned straight into the side of the Ferrari to eliminate Berger and himself. Gerhard's fault? René's fault? Or just a 'racing accident?' Whatever, the charisma of a possible second 1988 Ferrari win evaporated as Berger, knowing he'd have run out of fuel anyway, phlegmatically walked back to the paddock with Arnoux to take a helicopter to Adelaide airport. And that was the last we saw of the scarlet Turbo 'Chargers' because the unfortunate Michele Alboreto had ended his final drive for Maranello in similar circumstances when he was rammed by Alex Caffi's Dallara just after the start.

So situation normal at the front now. McLarens first and second with Prost ahead and Senna penalised by a faulty gearbox which had an unco-operative mind of its own. A dull remaining race then? Not a bit of it! Behind the leaders 1987 World Champion Nelson Piquet, in an unaccustomed third place, was having to work very hard indeed to stay ahead of the warring Williams of Patrese and Mansell, with Capelli chasing hard in sixth place. It was Riccardo's 176th Grand Prix (to equal Graham Hill and Jacques Laffite's record) and he'd never driven better. In the leading 3½ litre car it was only his inferior power on the long Brabham Straight that stopped him passing Piquet and, in an equal car, Mansell behind could do nothing about him.

Until lap 53 when, succumbing to Nigel's ceaseless pressure, Riccardo half-spun. Nigel was past in a flash to catch and harry his unloved rival Piquet. But if Patrese couldn't pass Nelson neither could Nigel and, on lap 66, his over-stressed brakes, suspect from the beginning, said 'enough'. The Williams was into the wall and a limping Mansell was out of his last race for Frank. A sad departure after 13 wins with the team.

Seven laps earlier the superb Prost, never putting a wheel wrong and driving with the usual effortless fluidity which belies his speed, had made the quickest of a succession of fastest laps (1m 21.216s = 103.870 mph) and with a lead of nearly 30 seconds over the hampered Senna he had lapped the fifth-placed man — Andrea De Cesaris. Now Andrea takes a lot of stick from the media for his erractic driving but when he is in the mood he can go really well — and today he was flying. He'd advanced from 15th on the grid to catch and pass, amongst others, Boutsen, Capelli and Warwick, and they don't hang about! What a pity then that, in his last drive for the little German Rial team he ran out of petrol with only four laps between himself and his second points finish of the season.

But Andrea wasn't alone in his misfortune. Adelaide maintained its grisly reputation as driver after driver spun, crashed, ran out of petrol, broke down or otherwise eliminated himself from the final race of the year, and there were only seven cars running when it finished. Nakajima ran into Gugelmin. Palmer's transmission packed up. Warwick and Cheever's Megatron engines blew themselves into oblivion. Modena and Larrauri's driveshafts broke. The Benetton twins of Nannini and Boutsen both spun although Thierry hauled himself into a fifth-place points finish with a stuttering engine. Capelli punctured but finished sixth. Johansson so close to his first point of the year, and Alliot retired with dry tanks and Alex Caffi's clutch failed.

Only the first four went the distance — Prost, Senna, Piquet and Patrese followed, a lap down, by Boutsen and Capelli — and only eleven were classified as finishers.

So ended the turbo era with Honda-power fittingly taking the first three places, ahead

Race 16 — AUSTRALIA

Name the guilty man!

139

Alain's second Australian GP win — and one of the best of his record 35 victories.

of three 'atmospheric' cars. Once again Grand Prix racing had shown itself to be a technological hothouse which forces development at an almost break-neck speed and once again the designers had demonstrated their ability to outwit the rule-makers' efforts to slow down Formula One. But, in a situation where turbocharging had massively escalated the already frightening costs of Grand Prix racing without any real benefit to spectators and viewers, their passing would be mourned by few.

Adelaide 1988 finished on a controversial note — Prost wound up the season with a record 105 points by finishing first or second in every race he completed. But he was beaten in the Championship by Senna, who scored 94 points which included a fourth and sixth place. No complaints from Prost, who accepts the 'best eleven scores from 16 races' rule but, as one who has to try to communicate it to the public, I can tell you that most people find it difficult to understand — time for a change?

AUSTRALIAN GRAND PRIX

Winner: Alain Prost, McLaren-Honda MP4/4-06   *Fastest Lap:* Alain Prost, 103.870 mph

GRID POSITION			RESULTS			WORLD CHAMPIONSHIP			
No.	Driver	Pos.	Driver	Car		Drivers	Pts	Constructors	Pts
12	Senna	1	Prost	McLaren-Honda MP4/4-06	1.	Senna	90*	1. McLaren-Honda	199
11	Prost	2	Senna	McLaren-Honda MP4/4-02	2.	Prost	87*	2. Ferrari	65
5	Mansell	3	Piquet	Lotus-Honda 100T/2	3.	Berger	41	3. Benetton-Ford	46†
28	Berger	4	Patrese	Williams-Judd FW12/3	4.	Boutsen	31†	4. Lotus-Honda	21
1	Piquet	5	Boutsen	Benetton-Ford B188-08	5.	Alboreto	24	5. Arrows-Megatron	20
6	Patrese	6	Capelli	March-Judd 881/5	6.	Piquet	20	March-Judd	20
17	Warwick	7	Martini	Minardi-Cosworth M188-05	7.	Capelli	15	Williams-Judd	20
19	Nannini	8	De Cesaris	Rial-Cosworth ARC1/01		Nannini	15	8. Tyrrell-Cosworth	5
16	Capelli	9	Johansson	Ligier-Judd JS31/04		Warwick	15	9. Rial-Cosworth	3
20	Boutsen	10	Alliot	Lola-Cosworth LC88-03	10.	Mansell	12	10. Minardi-Cosworth	1
36	Caffi	11	Streiff	AGS-Cosworth JH23/4	11.	Patrese	8		
27	Alboreto				12.	Cheever	5		
2	Nakajima					Gugelmin	5		
23	Martini					Palmer	5		
22	De Cesaris				15.	De Cesaris	3		
14	Streiff				16.	Martini	1		
3	Palmer					Nakajima	1		
18	Cheever								
15	Gugelmin				*Points total counting best 11 results only.				
33	Modena				†Points total subject to official confirmation.				
24	Sala								
26	Johansson								
25	Arnoux								
30	Alliot								
32	Larrauri								
9	Ghinzani								

Review of 1988

When FISA, the governing body of motor sport, decided that Turbocars were getting too fast and potentially too dangerous, they revised the rules to phase them out over a two year period. In 1987, the turbos were allowed four-bar boost and 195 litres of fuel, an intended advantage over the normally-aspirated 3½ litre cars which turned out to be the reality — non-turbo cars took only eleven out of a possible 96 points-scoring places, and not one driver from this group even made it to the rostrum.

In 1988, restrictions were placed on turbocars which were designed to even up the racing. Via pop-off valves, turbo-boost was restricted to 2½ bar, and the maximum fuel allowance was reduced to 150 litres. Car weight too was a factor — a minimum of 540kg was set for the turbos, whereas for the normally-aspirated cars, the weight minimum was set at 500kg. With no fuel restrictions placed on the atmospheric cars, and no turbo-lag problems, it was predicted by many that Grand Prix racing in 1988 would be very competitive. 'They' reckoned without the dreaded 'Ronda' factor — Ron Dennis and Honda!

For 1988 was the year of McLaren-Honda,

Judd Marched on in 1988 — engine supplier John Judd and March team boss Ian Phillips — a happy combination.

1989 Italian jobs — over the moon? Nannini takes the Benetton No. 1 spot seriously. Over the Hill? Patrese is set to pass Graham Hill's 176 Grands Prix record.

the team which broke every record in the book with a car and an organisation which proved well-nigh invincible. Fifteen wins from sixteen races. Ten first and second places. Ten fastest laps. Fifteen pole positions. Twelve starting grid front rows. First and second places in the Drivers' World Championship. The Constructors' World Championship with a record number of points which was over twice as many as the next best. There had never been a year like it.

So what was their secret? Put simply, none of the other teams were able to put together an *overall* package to match the total strength of McLaren's. And who was responsible for masterminding the McLaren effort? Ron Dennis. For it was Ron who evolved and structured the 'strength-in-depth' McLaren organisation with its emphasis on teamwork rather than individual genius. Ron, who made sure that the team comprised the right sort of people. Ron who, over a period of years, 'cosied up' to Honda to enable his team to exploit their engine superiority. Ron who recruited Ayrton Senna to join the world's finest race driver, Alain Prost. Ron who also recruited the seemingly immovable Gordon Murray from Brabham, to replace the seemingly indispensable John Barnard as technical supremo. And Ron who drummed up vast amounts of money — the other really indispensable element for any successful team. 'My job here' he will tell you, 'is to make sure that everything works properly.' And he does just that. Some people say that being with McLaren is all efficiency and no fun but I haven't noticed any miserable faces there! With the superb facilities at Woking at

141

A rare smile from a superb World Champion — Ayrton Senna will be number 1 in the programmes for '89.

his disposal, Steve Nichols designed the first totally new McLaren since John Barnard's all-conquering original MP4 and the result, powered by Honda, driven by Prost and Senna, tyred by Goodyear, backed by stunningly smooth-running organisation and administration, and supported by their sponsors' willingness and ability to spend what it took, made every race seem a foregone conclusion.

For me, apart from McLaren, the teams of the year were March and Benetton. Robin Herd's March Company, with financial backing from the Japanese Leyton House Organisation, made a very welcome, comparatively low-key, one-car return to Grand Prix racing in 1987, using what was basically a development of their previous year's Formula 3000 car driven by the very promising Ivan Capelli. Encouraged by their 'learning' year and with Leyton House saying 'get in there' financially, they moved up several gears in 1988 — with great success. Their super-slippery new car, designed by the talented (brilliant would be a better description actually) Adrian Newey and powered by John Judd's atmospheric V8, was a knock-out. Their resident joker Ivan Capelli's drives, particularly in the latter half of the season, were amongst the very best of the year. Mauricio Gugelmin demonstrated real talent too but the thing that endeared the Team most of all to me was their infectious spirit of fun. They get the job done as well as any of their rivals and really seem to be enjoying it. But then with a bloke like Ian Phillips in charge it would be difficult not to!

Raise a glass to the Champions! McLaren reigned in Spain — and pretty well everywhere else.

It's the same at Benetton. If you can actually communicate with anyone in their garage above the noise of the ever-present 'ghetto-blaster' you can be sure that it will be a cheerful and informative conversation. Rory Byrne couldn't design a bad car if he tried to, and his 1988 package was as good as ever with sharp handling and extremely effective aerodynamics. The Ford DFR engine (the much-vaunted five valve version of which never actually materialised. Or if it did, no-one said so!) got better and better as the season progressed.

The greatest disappointment of 1988 surely has to be Lotus and it really was very sad to see this once truly great team with its historical background of multiple Drivers' and Constructors' Championships failing to succeed in spite of having Honda-power and three-times World Champion Nelson Piquet. Without being on the inside of the organisation it is difficult to know exactly what went so wrong, that a man who had won twenty Grands Prix with two other teams could be so far off the pace. To me it is inconceivable that blame can be attributed to Honda. Their support of Lotus seemed to be just as strong and enthusiastic as their support of McLaren, and doing well matters to them far too much to promote one team at the expense of the other. Which leaves two other factors — the drivers and the chassis. Intelligent consideration suggests that it was a bit of both. There is no doubt that Gerard Ducarouge's 100T chassis for Nelson and Naka wasn't anything like as effective as Steve Nichols' MP4/4 for Alain and Ayrton and that being so, even Piquet couldn't get it to the front. Informed comment suggested that Nelson had lost the motivation to push. He seldom criticised his Lotus but something was clearly amiss with the combination.

Williams, having been fired by Honda at the end of the '87 season, suffered both from having to learn the ways of their new atmospheric Judd V8 engine, and a reactive suspension system which was neither perfect nor popular with the team's drivers. Arrows were never likely to beat McLaren with their elderly four cylinder BMW-based Megatron turbo engines whilst for Ligier, 1988 was disastrous — at no time did they

Lotus positions for Gerard Ducarouge and Nelson Piquet — unfortunately they weren't winning ones.

look competitive and there were times when the cars almost seemed to have minds of their own.

The next major let-down for me was Ferrari. At the end of 1987 they'd come good with convincing wins in Japan and Australia after two years in the wilderness. With John Barnard supposedly firmly in the technical saddle and with the need just to 'detune' their fine V6 turbo engine following their decision to stay with their excellent 187 chassis they were firmly expected to be winners in '88 — especially with 'charger' Gerhard Berger and the experienced and talented Michele Alboreto to drive for them. But their engine men let them down badly. Except at Monza on that charismatic day, and perhaps inspired by the memory of their great founder, when they came home first and second after the late race collision with Schlesser cost Senna a certain victory.

In short, they were all outclassed. The expertise, experience, expenditure and sheer effort that the Japanese concern puts into its Grand Prix involvement coupled with identical commitment from McLaren meant that where other teams were weak McLaren-Honda were strong. Because they were strong everywhere.

So on the driver front who are now the best? In terms of proven ability and their performances during the season, they have to be Berger, Mansell, Prost and Senna. But in what order? Well with his overall record and his 1988 success, it has to be Senna first — a mere whisker ahead of Prost, but ahead nevertheless. Ayrton's magnificent drive in Japan made him World Champion and never was the honour more deserved. He broke virtually every record in the achievements book but in my opinion it wasn't so much what he did but the way he did it that made him so outstanding. His dedication and application is almost frightening and when you ally that to his supreme driving talent, ruthless aggression, absolute determination and the best car, it is hardly surprising that the only other driver who could rival him was his team-mate Alain Prost. Now that Ayrton has achieved his fiercely-held ambition maybe he will be a bit more relaxed and outgoing. It would be welcome, but in any case he will be a World Champion to be proud of.

Prost is the first to admit that he was outdriven by Senna during 1988 but his achievements speak for themselves and would handsomely have won him his third Championship in any other year. He certainly has nothing to reproach himself about. For me he is still the most complete driver of them all but 1989 will be a testing year for him now that Senna has the psychological advantage.

I find it very hard to separate Mansell and Berger both of whom drove some superb races during 1988 in cars which were not winners. But driven to the wall and taking jolly good care not to be seen anywhere near the Isle of Man, I'd place Berger at Number Three with Nigel a hair'sbreadth behind him.

Of the rest I've special plaudits for three — Thierry Boutsen, Alessandro Nannini and Ivan Capelli. Boutsen is such a quiet and self-effacing chap (and a charming one, too) that he tends to get overlooked. But his performances during the season in a car which was most unlikely ever to beat the McLarens, were altogether outstanding. Third place after third place with a smooth and unobtrusive style which reflected his personality. If the Renault V10 engine propels next year's Williams as fast as he hopes it will, he's got what it takes to win in 1989. And so has Alessandro Nannini. Like Boutsen, third places were the best he could realistically hope for and he got them. As team leader to Johnny Herbert, he is another man who will be up-front next year if Ford's exclusive-for-Benetton new V8 is up to the job.

And then the mercurial Ivan Capelli. What a star! Not just an absolutely brilliant talent at the wheel but such a refreshing personality out of the cockpit. As I've said before the March team uniquely allies ability with fun and a lot of that is down to Ivan who openly enjoys his racing — which is a lot more than you can say for some of his rivals who perpetually moan about their privileged lot. His superb drives in Portugal and Spain, and his breathtaking if shortlived lead in Japan ensured that he will be a 'watched' man in 1989.

It's in the nature of an enthusiast to be optimistic about the future and I'm certainly optimistic about next season. It's all new in 1989. New rules. Turbos out. Everyone with normally-aspirated engines. The glorious sounds of V12 Ferraris, V10 Honda-powered McLarens and Renault-powered Williams racing against the host of V8 motivated teams — amongst them Benetton, Arrows, Lotus, Tyrrell, Zakspeed (with Yamaha engines), March and Dallara. Amazingly having a loss of at least 200 horsepower this year made virtually no difference to race and lap speeds thanks to aerodynamic and handling developments and no 'excess horsepower' wheelspin. Next year they'll be matching and even exceeding 1987 speeds. Technology defeats FISA!

With every team having to field two cars in 1989 and with some very impressive new outfits trying to get into Formula One the racing is going to be faster, more competitive, more varied, more interesting and more exciting than ever. Roll on!